World Prospects
for Natural Resources

Some Projections of Demand
and Indicators of Supply
to the Year 2000

World Prospects for Natural Resources

Some Projections of Demand and Indicators of Supply to the Year 2000

By JOSEPH L. FISHER
and NEAL POTTER

RESOURCES FOR THE FUTURE, INC.,
1755 Massachusetts Avenue, N.W., Washington, D.C., 20036

Distributed by THE JOHNS HOPKINS PRESS,
Baltimore and London

RESOURCES FOR THE FUTURE, INC.
1755 Massachusetts Avenue, N.W., Washington, D.C. 20036

Board of Directors: Erwin D. Canham, *Chairman*, Robert O. Anderson, Harrison Brown, Edward J. Cleary, Joseph L. Fisher, Luther H. Foster, F. Kenneth Hare, Charles J. Hitch, Charles F. Luce, Frank Pace, Jr., William S. Paley, Emanuel R. Piore, Stanley H. Ruttenberg, Lauren K. Soth, P. F. Watzek, Gilbert F. White.

Honorary Directors: Horace M. Albright, Reuben G. Gustavson, Hugh L. Keenleyside, Edward S. Mason, Leslie A. Miller, Laurance S. Rockefeller, John W. Vanderwilt.

President: Joseph L. Fisher
Vice President: Michael F. Brewer
Secretary-Treasurer: John E. Herbert

Resources for the Future is a nonprofit corporation for research and education in the development, conservation, and use of natural resources and the improvement of the quality of the environment. It was established in 1952 with the cooperation of the Ford Foundation. Part of the work of Resources for the Future is carried out by its resident staff; part is supported by grants to universities and other nonprofit organizations. Unless otherwise stated, interpretations and conclusions in RFF publications are those of the authors; the organization takes responsibility for the selection of significant subjects for study, the competence of the researchers, and their freedom of inquiry.

RFF editors: Henry Jarrett, Vera W. Dodds, Nora E. Roots, Tadd Fisher.

Copyright © 1964 by Resources for the Future, Inc., Washington, D.C.
All rights reserved
Manufactured in the United States of America

ISBN-0-8018-0197-4

Paperback edition, 1964
Second printing, 1966
Third printing, 1970

NOTE: An earlier, shorter version of this study was presented to the Twenty-third American Assembly in May, 1963. That paper, entitled "Resources in the United States and the World," by Joseph L. Fisher and Neal Potter, was subsequently published by Prentice-Hall, Inc., Englewood Cliffs, N.J., as a chapter in *The Population Dilemma*, Philip M. Hauser, editor, copyright 1963 by The American Assembly, Columbia University, New York City. The authors are grateful for the permission of Prentice-Hall and The American Assembly to use the original material in this revised, more detailed version.

Contents

1. THE QUESTION OF RESOURCE ADEQUACY 1
   What the Indicators Can Show 3
   Principal Points to Be Covered 5

2. THE CASE OF THE UNITED STATES 7
   Per Capita Consumption 8
   Employment per Unit of Output 9
   Relative Costs and Prices 12
   Net Imports 14
   Reserves and Potentials for Meeting Requirements 17

3. WORLD TRENDS IN RESOURCES 20
   Consumption or Output 20
   Employment/Output Ratio 30
   Relative Price Trends 32
   Net Import Trends 34
   Conclusion 38

4. PROJECTIONS OF RESOURCE DEMANDS 40
   Food Products 41
   Energy Commodities 46
   Nonfuel Minerals 48
   Forest Products 50

5. RESERVES AND ALTERNATE
   SUPPLY POSSIBILITIES 51
   Food 52
   Energy 58
   Metallic Minerals 60
   Forest Products 61
   Water 62

6. SOME CONCLUDING OBSERVATIONS 66

LIST OF TABLES

Table 1. Requirements of Selected Natural Resources and Resource Products, 1960 and Projected 2000 18
Table 2. Food: Per Capita Production by World Areas, Prewar to 1960 21
Table 3. Food: Calorie Consumption Per Capita by World Areas, Prewar to 1960-61 23
Table 4. Energy: Per Capita Consumption by World Areas, 1929 to 1960 26
Table 5. Iron Ore: Total Output by World Areas, 1937 to 1960 28
Table 6. Copper Output by World Areas, 1937 to 1960 29
Table 7. Total Wood Removals by World Areas, 1946 to 1960 31
Table 8. Changes in Employment/Output Ratios for Agriculture and Mining 33
Table 9. Indexes of World Prices of Selected Resource Commodities, 1900 to 1960 35
Table 10. Net Imports, Food and Feed, 1934-38 to 1960...... 37
Table 11. Population Trends: Historical 1920-1960, and Projections 1980 and 2000, by World Areas 42
Table 12. Projections of Calorie Consumption in the Year 2000 Compared to 1960 Actual for World Areas 44
Table 13. Projections of Energy Consumed in 2000 Compared to 1960 Actual by World Areas 47
Table 14. Changes in Crop Yields per Acre, by Major Crops for Selected World Areas 53

LIST OF FIGURES

Figure 1. U.S. Resource Sectors: Per Capita Consumption, 1870-1960 8
Figure 2. U.S. Resource Sectors: Employment/Output, 1870-1960 10
Figure 3. All U.S. Resources and Major Sectors: Employment/Output Relative to Manufacturing, 1870-1960 11
Figure 4. U.S. Resource Sectors: Deflated Prices, 1870-1960 .. 13
Figure 5. U.S. Foreign Trade in Resource Commodities as Percent of Domestic Consumption, 1870-1960 16
Figure 6. Estimated Values of Food Supplies Per Capita by World Regions, Prewar to 1958-60 24

CHAPTER

I

The Question of Resource Adequacy

The question of natural resource adequacy has always been significant; it will not become less so in the future. Throughout history people have been concerned about the relationship between themselves and the land and other resources available to them. As geographic boundaries of regions and continents became known, and as statistical trends of population and agricultural production became established, this concern found more sophisticated and comprehensive expression. Malthus propounded one far-reaching proposition: population tends to outrun the means of subsistence, making preventive checks to population increase desirable and ultimately positive checks necessary. However, the working out of the consequences of the industrial revolution so increased the output of goods and services that Malthus' gloomy prediction has not come true, at least in the Western world.

In more recent times the "population explosion" in the underdeveloped countries and very rapid increases in most of the more developed places have led to a reawakening of concern about the capacity of the natural environment and its resources to sustain desired rates of economic growth. Science, technology, and the economic adaption of their accomplishments are seen as pitted against the sheer increase of population, which in many less developed areas is now running at 3 per cent a year. Continuation of this rate would mean a doubling every twenty-four years.

Clearly the population problem is not simply one of numbers of people, but also of natural resources and how they are used. Much light can be thrown on this concept by trying to project resource trends into the future and bringing them into juxtaposition with population trends. Of key importance in determining the outcome of the population-resources (or man-land) situation are the prevailing levels of technology and culture, including organizational and institutional elements. Population projections, from Malthus to those of the recent past, have been notoriously wide of the mark. Projections of natural resources, if anything, have been worse, largely because of the difficulties of projecting technology and institutional adjustments. Nevertheless, some understanding may come from a look at comparative trends in the past, present levels of resource use, and at a few projections into the future even though the projections have to be strictly hypothetical and are altogether a hazardous and uncertain undertaking.

We shall examine resource problems principally in terms of certain indicators of whether natural resources and resource products are becoming scarcer in the United States and other major countries of the world. Five indicators of scarcity will be examined:

1) Production and/or consumption trends for major resource products, especially per capita trends. Special attention will be given to food and energy.

2) Employment per unit of output, as a measure of labor productivity trends in resource industries.

3) Relative price and/or cost trends for resource commodities as compared to trends of prices and/or costs in general.

4) Trends in exports and imports, or net foreign trade.

5) Trends in the rate of production and use of resources compared to estimated stocks, reserves, or potentials.

WHAT THE INDICATORS CAN SHOW

At the start, a few general observations may help to clarify the relationships between these indicators and the problem of scarcity.

First, scarcity in the most obvious sense always increases as population grows, for the physical content of the globe never changes significantly, and scarcity might thus be defined as the reciprocal of population. Such a definition of scarcity puts aside most problems of interest or significance, however, and points ultimately to the absurd conclusion that the Red Indians were better off materially before 1492 than Americans are today.

The actual output or consumption of resource commodities, stated in per capita terms, provides a crude measure of "welfare." This, however, takes no account of the cost or effort of obtaining supplies. The relationship between the labor inputs and the outputs of resource commodities gives a measure of the human cost of making resources available for consumption. This is the measure to which Malthus and the classical economists devoted their attention; it was their expectations of a rise in the labor cost of food and other resource commodities that led them to a gloomy view of a world with increasing population.

It may be argued that advances in technology rather than increases in the plenitude of resources account for declines in the ratio of labor input to resource output. This, of course, may be true, but as long as this process continues, scarcity of resources cannot become a threat to the level of living. It is also of interest that the ratio between labor inputs and outputs in the resource industries has not only declined, but has done so in the United States at a rate nearly the same as that in manufacturing, in which resource scarcity poses very few direct problems.[1]

Labor inputs per unit of output reflect not only technology and availability of resources, but also capital inputs and inputs of fuel, fertilizer, and other materials. For this reason the relative prices of resource commodities, which reflect the costs of all inputs relative to the general price level, are useful as a check on the trend of employment/output ratios.

In addition, the percentage of consumption supplied by net imports is significant, since in many cases imports relieve the pressure for higher prices and employment/output ratios which increasing scarcity would otherwise cause. It must be remembered, however, that this measure too is incomplete, for it is "comparative advantage" which directs the flow of foreign trade: the ratio of the costs of domestic and foreign resource industries, compared to the ratio of the costs at home and abroad for the nonresource industries. Thus, either a discovery of low-cost oil in Venezuela or a rise in the efficiency of an American manufacturing industry that would make it more attractive than domestic extraction of natural resources could account for a rise in U.S. oil imports; and tariffs, quotas, and monopolies also play their part.

Finally, one may compare the trends in the rate of use of resources with estimates of stocks or reserves. This would perhaps be the most satisfactory test of scarcity, but it is

---

[1] Neal Potter and Francis T. Christy, Jr., *Trends in Natural Resource Commodities* (Baltimore: The Johns Hopkins Press for Resources for the Future, 1962), pp. 15–16.

The Question of Resource Adequacy

just here that the data are most unsatisfactory. Ultimate reserves of most materials are many times larger than are likely to be used in the foreseeable future; and the limitations on resources available in the near future are not fixed, but highly dependent on the technologies and prices which one projects for that future, so that we are carried back to our second and third indicators, labor productivity trends and relative cost or price trends.

We shall examine insofar as possible the statistics for all of the five indicators outlined above. No one of them is sufficient by itself to give a well-rounded picture of increasing or decreasing scarcity; together they shed a good deal of light on the matter even though they cannot prove conclusively the case for or against scarcity. They are indicators to be used cautiously and to be improved.

PRINCIPAL POINTS TO BE COVERED

In Chapter 2 the examination of the five resource scarcity indicators is made for the United States, for which reasonably good data relating to the five indicators are available. In Chapter 3 we examine the data that are available for continental areas of the world and for selected countries. As will be seen, these data are sketchy and uncertain, but we use them as best we can to throw light on the trends of world resource scarcity. Also this procedure will show the additions and improvements in data that will be required if speculations about future demand for resources are to become more useful.

Following this, in Chapter 4, demand for a number of resource commodities is projected to the year 2000 for the world and for certain regions and countries. The resource demands are related to population and productivity trends primarily, and are carried forward on the basis of trends and several hypothetical patterns of improvement in levels of living in various parts of the world. Demand estimates for intervening years, 1980 for example, can be interpolated to give a rough approximation of the possible situation less far ahead.

Projections beyond the year 2000 are not attempted because the degree of error in assumptions about population, productivity of agriculture, mineral reserves, technology, and other essentials is too large to be dealt with in a study of this kind.

Chapter 5 is a brief survey of resource reserves and supply alternatives. New discoveries of sources of supply plus technological advance in substitutes and reduction of waste bear importantly on the question of scarcity.

Finally, in Chapter 6, we make certain concluding observations on the direction of policies and social adjustments suggested by this kind of advance reading of trends toward or away from resource scarcity. The poor condition of the data, which justifies only the simplest kinds of projection methods, means that policy observations have to be tentative. We hope, however, that this monograph will help indicate trends and problems as well as data and analyses needed for better policy conclusions.

CHAPTER

2

The Case of the United States

It is self-evident that natural resources and their immediately derived products and services are essential to economic growth and well-being. Enough of these things must be available within a country or by way of imports. In a more highly developed country such as the United States, dependence upon resources may not always be obvious because of the overlay of processed items and the variety of economic services with no very close connection with resources. But the ultimate dependence on natural resources remains, never far below the surface. Many particular resources are a wasting asset; discovery of new sources and the development of substitutes may continue to avert the consequences of this characteristic, but for how long no one can say for certain.

Depite the possibility of altogether new developments, the history of what has happened in the past remains our most reliable guide to future likelihood. Statistics that trace the trends of production, consumption, prices, productivity and net foreign trade have recently been assembled for resource commodities of the United States.[1] The data from 1870 to the present are reasonably consistent and reliable and can be used in applying the first four indicators of scarcity mentioned in the preceding chapter.

[1] Neal Potter and Francis T. Christy, Jr., *Trends in Natural Resource Commodities*.

PER CAPITA CONSUMPTION

The first indicator of resource scarcity or abundance in the United States is provided by the historical trend of consumption of resource commodities on a per capita basis. Figure 1 shows the trends from 1870 to 1960 for the major

FIGURE 1. U.S. Resource Sectors: Per Capita Consumption, 1870–1960

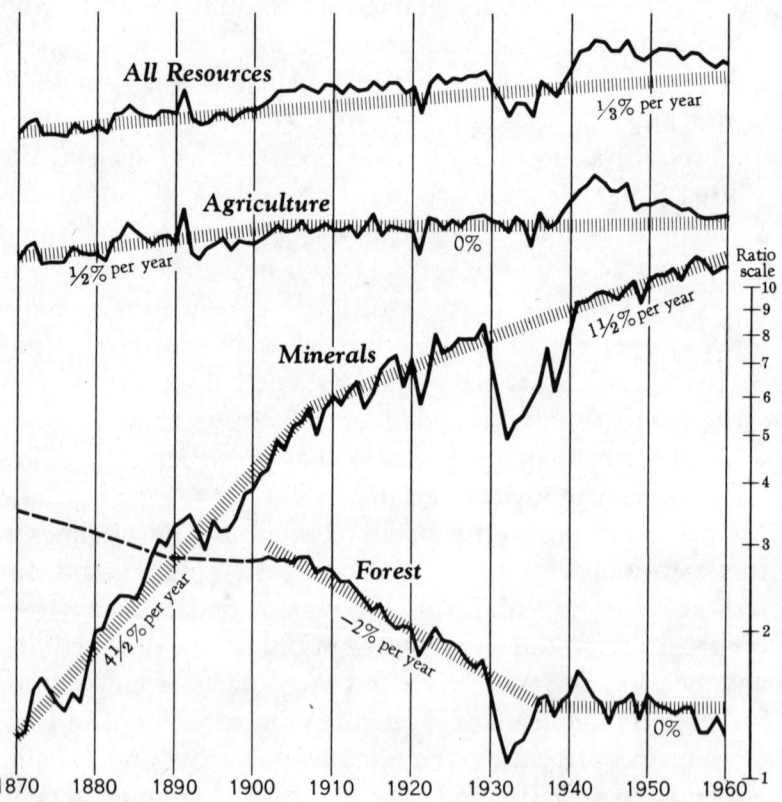

Source: Neal Potter and Francis T. Christy, Jr., *Trends in Natural Resource Commodities* (Baltimore: The Johns Hopkins Press for Resources for the Future, 1962), Chart 23.

resource categories. The over-all trend appears to be steadily upward; only for forest products has the trend been downward.

The aggregates cover up much significant detail. Within the minerals category, for example, oil, natural gas, bauxite for aluminum, and other items have risen steeply, while anthracite and bituminous coal have declined generally since the First World War period. Among the agricultural products, per capita consumption of wheat and hogs has fallen over the ninety years, while beef, milk products, and notably citrus fruits have risen. Lumber has declined; pulp and paper have increased.

In terms of the amount of resource products consumed by each man, woman, and child in the United States over nearly a century, scarcity has not been increasing. Instead it has decreased persistently at about 1/3 of 1 per cent a year, with the only major interruption occurring in the early 1930's.

EMPLOYMENT PER UNIT OF OUTPUT

The second indicator is the real cost of resource goods and services in terms of labor productivity. Over the years for which reasonably good statistics are available, has the cost in human effort of making resource products and services available to the American economy been increasing or not?

The employment/output ratio[2] for the resource or extractive industries taken as a whole has been falling consist-

---

[2] We use the employment/output ratio instead of the usual output/employment (productivity) ratio because we are concerned with the real cost of obtaining a certain output in terms of labor input and with the factors underlying changes in real prices.

ently for many decades with only an occasional and short-lived interruption. Since the mid-1930's the downward trend has been particularly marked. This has been true of each of the major resource categories with the notable exception of forest products and possibly also of fish. Increases in productivity in agriculture and mining have outstripped those in manufacturing during the past twenty-five years or so. Figures 2 and 3 summarize these trends.

FIGURE 2. U.S. Resource Sectors: Employment/Output, 1870–1960

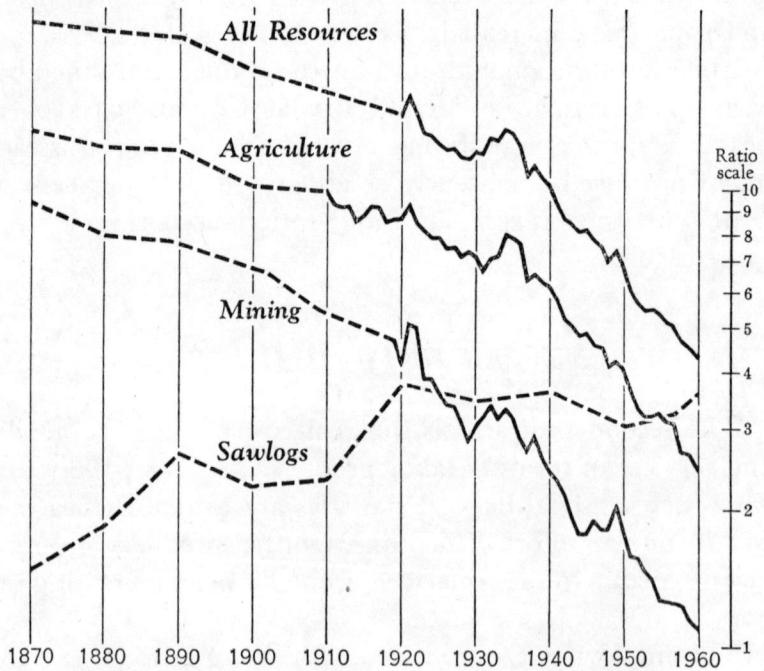

Note: The dashed lines indicate periods for which the data are available less frequently than on an annual basis.

Source: Potter and Christy, Chart 45. (For full source reference see Figure 1.)

FIGURE 3. All U.S. Resources and Major Sectors:
Employment/Output Relative to Manufacturing

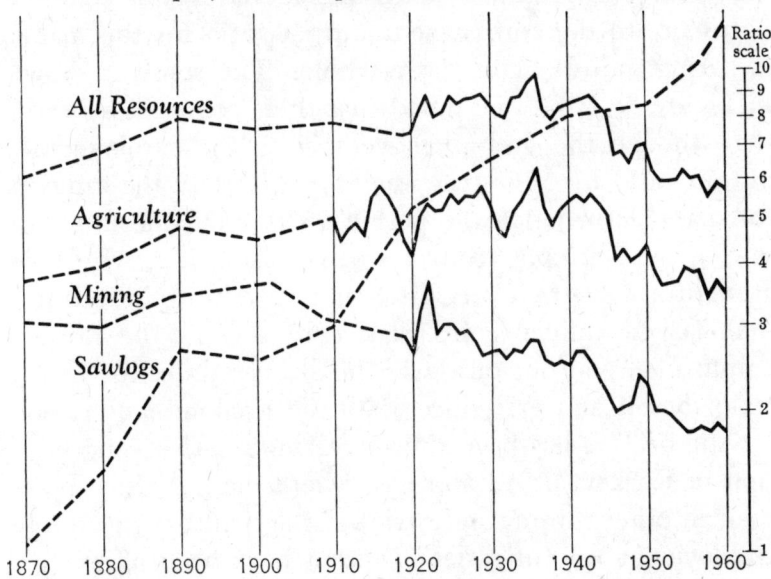

Source: Potter and Christy, Chart 47. (For full source reference, see Figure 1.)

The number of workers engaged in all the resource industries was just about the same in 1960 as in 1870, 7 million. But the value of their output in constant dollars had increased by more than five times. During the same long period the value of the total national product rose by more than twenty times, with more complex fabrication of raw materials and a larger services component in the expanding economy. About 10 per cent of the nation's labor force, instead of over 50 per cent as in 1870, was producing 20 per cent more in resource products for each member of the population.

While this simple measure is a significant indicator of diminished scarcity, it is well to see whether scarcity of supplies has made the progress of the resource industries slower than it would have been otherwise. To do this, we compare the changes in employment/output ratios for resource industries to the employment/output ratio for the manufacturing industry taken as a whole. The result is shown in Figure 3. It will be noted that these comparisons show that, though the over-all movement in the employment/output ratio for resources was approximately the same as for manufacturing in the period 1870–1960, the ratio for sawlogs rose steeply relative to manufacturing, while for agriculture it moved very little, and for mining it declined. The largest influence in relative decline in the mining employment/output ratio was the estimated decline in the ratio for oil and gas; since 1930 the predominant reason for the decline has been the increasing relative concentration of workers in oil and gas, where they produce more than in other mining industries. In agriculture, declining employment/output ratios for crops have been offset by a rise in the ratios for beef and pork relative to the ratios in manufacturing.

According to this indicator—how much work it takes to produce resource products and services—resources are not becoming scarcer; on the contrary, more is being produced with less labor; over a ninety-year period the gain has been at about as rapid a pace as in manufacturing.

RELATIVE COSTS AND PRICES

The third indicator is the relative cost or price trend. If a resource is becoming scarcer, one would expect the cost of developing or producing resource products derived from it to rise in comparison with costs generally. Over the long run, prices usually reflect costs fairly accurately. Because price data are easier to come by than cost data, they can be used as a measure of both relative cost and price. Statistics in the early period are not thoroughly reliable, but the general picture which emerges, as shown in Figure 4, is that for extractive industries as a whole, prices have not shown any marked tendency to rise or fall over the long run since 1870. They have moved erratically with many short-term ups and downs and possibly some slight general tendency upward. The component to move upward most noticeably

FIGURE 4. U.S. Resource Sectors: Deflated Prices, 1870–1960

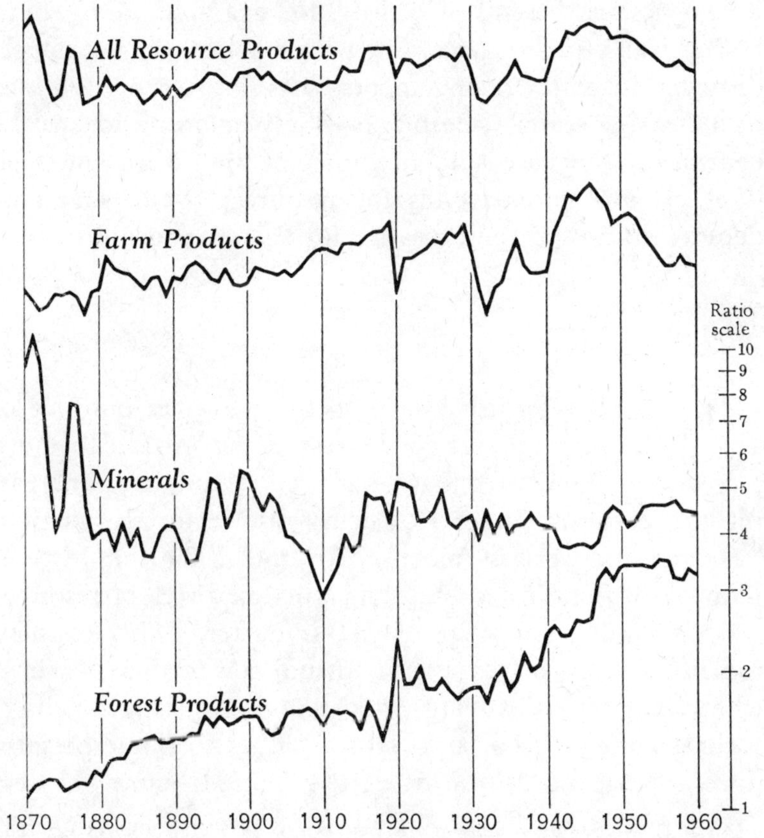

Source: Potter and Christy, Chart 1. (For full source reference see Figure 1.)

has been forest products, for which relative prices recently have been nearly four times what they were in 1870 and twice those in 1930, although they have not risen particularly since the late 1940's.

But the overall picture does not indicate that resource materials have become scarcer on any general or alarming scale over a good many decades in the past. Technological and economic factors underlying increases in efficiency have largely offset tendencies toward greater difficulties and higher costs of extraction. A detailed examination of the long-term price trend of copper, for example, after eliminating war years and years in which prices were seriously distorted by cartel arrangements, does not support the idea of increasing scarcity, despite a widely held opinion to the contrary.[3] The past is no guarantee of the future, but relative cost and price trends for resources over many past decades do not portend disaster for the next few.

NET IMPORTS

The fourth indicator relates to the resources position of a single country relative to the rest of the world. In more recent years the United States has been relying to an increasing degree upon imports of many raw materials, particularly oil and certain metals. Around 1930 the historic position of the United States as a net exporter of resource products shifted to that of net importer. This country continues to export basic agricultural commodities such as wheat and cotton, and to import noncompeting products such as coffee, cocoa, and natural rubber. But especially since the Second World War, the United States has also

[3] Orris C. Herfindahl, *Copper Costs and Prices: 1870–1957* (Baltimore: The Johns Hopkins Press for Resources for the Future, 1959).

The Case of the United States

become a fairly large net importer of such items as crude oil, copper, lead, zinc, iron ore, and lumber; while its already considerable imports of manganese, nickel, chromium, asbestos, diamonds, and paper have continued upward. For the 1955–61 period imports of crude oil were 16 per cent of domestic consumption and imports of iron ore were 23 per cent.

Figure 5 shows the long-term trends of net trade as a per cent of consumption for all extractive industries and for agricultural and mineral products. Without increased imports of particular commodities, costs and prices of certain items in the United States would probably have risen (or have risen more than they did), especially since the Second World War. In some cases new sources or techniques undoubtedly set ceilings on both price rises and amount of imports; for example, oil can be produced from ample reserves of oil shale in the Colorado plateau at only a little above existing oil prices, and low-grade taconite ores, of which there are large reserves in the Lake states, can be beneficiated. Nevertheless, the fact remains that ready access to foreign supplies has gained in importance to this country.

Looked at from a national viewpoint and without detailed analysis, this indicator suggests decreasing plenitude of raw materials. From a world viewpoint it reflects only shifting currents of trade, due to changes in the comparative cost advantages of other industries as against raw materials production, both in the United States and in other countries. Government controls and subsidies also affect comparative advantages.

The other three tests indicate either lessening scarcity, or at least no increase in scarcity, for most items. There are some exceptions, notably lumber (sawlogs), among the more basic materials. Trends in per capita consumption of re-

FIGURE 5. U.S. Foreign Trade in Resource Commodities as Per Cent of Domestic Consumption

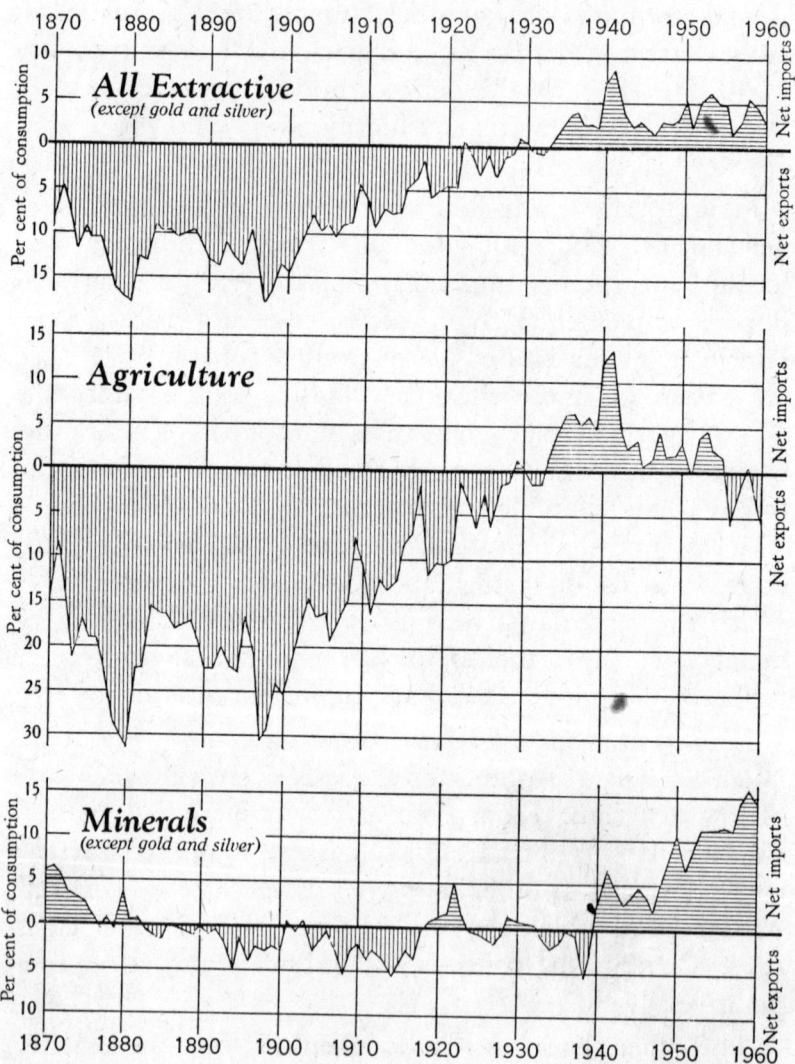

Source: Potter and Christy, Charts 34, 36, and 38. (For full source reference see Figure 1.)

source products, labor productivity trends, and deflated price and cost movements for raw materials—each of these seems to point to the unlikelihood of any general running out of resources in this country for some time to come.[4]

RESERVES AND POTENTIALS FOR MEETING REQUIREMENTS

The fifth indicator, necessarily more speculative than the others, involves the trend of rates of production and use of resources compared to estimates of stocks, reserves, or potentials. For the United States a recent comprehensive appraisal attempts to review the historical data and to look into the future in terms of foreseeable new sources of supply, new technology, population trends, and expectations for a rising level of living.[5] Based on an estimated increase in population from 180 million in 1960 to 330 million in 2000 and in gross national product in 1960 dollars from $504 billion in 1960 to $2,200 billion in 2000, and also taking into account other demand and supply factors related specifically to each item, Table 1 shows the projected increases in a few basic resource and raw material requirements.

In the study from which these estimates are taken, a range of requirements is presented: high, medium, and low. The figures in Table 1 are the medium estimates and should be regarded as projections on the basis of assump-

---

[4] Historical data on resource trends have been analyzed carefully in terms of resources-economic growth models in Harold J. Barnett and Chandler Morse, *Scarcity and Growth* (Baltimore: The Johns Hopkins Press for Resources for the Future, 1963).

[5] Hans H. Landsberg, Leonard L. Fischman, Joseph L. Fisher, *Resources in America's Future* (Baltimore: The Johns Hopkins Press for Resources for the Future, 1963).

TABLE 1. U.S. Requirements of Selected Natural Resources and Resource Products, 1960 and Projected 2000

	1960	2000
Cropland including pasture (million acres)	447	476
Wheat (million bushels)	1,110	1,385
Cotton (billion pounds)	7.0	16
Timber (billion cu. ft.)	11	32
Fresh water withdrawal depletions (billion gal. per day)	84	149
East	*13.7*	*37.4*
West	*59.7*	*91.7*
Pacific Northwest	*11.1*	*20.2*
Oil (billion bbls.)	3.2	10.0
Natural gas (trillion cu. ft.)	13.3	34.9
Coal (million short tons)	436	718
Nuclear power (billion kilowatt-hours)	—	2,400
Iron ore (million short tons)	131	341
Aluminum, primary (million short tons)	2.1	13.3
Copper, primary (million short tons))	1.7	4.5

Source: Landsberg, Fischman and Fisher. (See n. 5.)

tions of population, production, income, and the like which are as realistic as so broad an approach would allow.

Regarding ability of the economy to meet these demands, three summary comments may be made. (1) The record of the past is reassuring: resource stocks, reserves, and potentials have been quite adequate to support sizeable economic growth. Gross national product has increased much more than total resource consumption (twenty-one times for GNP, from 1870 to 1960, compared to six times for resource consumption). (2) Resource demands can be met through new discoveries, technical advances of many sorts, substitutions of cheaper and more plentiful materials, new investment, improved resource management and use, increased imports of certain items, and other activities. (3) As scarcity appears for any item, pressures will mount to circumvent the consequences; ultimately, if no other solution is found, the cost and price of the item will rise and force an accommodation.

More specifically, there apparently will be enough cropland, assuming yields per acre continue to increase in line with recent trends. Meeting the increased demand for lumber will strain the country's capacity to produce sawtimber; and probably the United States will have to resort to additional imports and further substitutions, especially during the latter part of the period between now and 2000. Improved management of forests and use of products will also be desirable. Water problems are primarily regional; their solution will require more investment in conserving and developing supplies and reducing pollution, and more efficient management and use. Petroleum, now in oversupply here and in the world generally, may be short toward the end of the century. Fortunately there are good possibilities of supplementing underground liquid sources with oil shale and tar sands. Coal reserves remain plentiful. Very large nuclear sources await further reductions in cost. Costs of extracting and refining many nonfuel minerals are high, even though the minerals themselves are abundant in the earth's crust. But many areas of the world from which imports can be obtained have not been very well explored, some not at all, and the possibilities of using lower grade ores are reasonably bright based on the U.S. experience of recent years. For the minerals especially, it will be important to this country that import capacity is not reduced and that technological progress continues.

CHAPTER

3

World Trends
in Resources

Having taken this glimpse at the relatively complete historical picture available for the United States, we shall now look at selected statistical information available for other countries and areas of the world which in most instances is far more limited. We shall seek to use the world data to construct the scarcity indicators surveyed in the preceding section for the United States, recognizing both the paucity and poor quality of much of the data for many other parts of the world. In this and the following section the discussion is confined largely to continents and world areas; the accompanying tables show data for selected major countries within the larger areas.

CONSUMPTION OR OUTPUT

Food. In the critical area of food production, it is encouraging to find a Food and Agriculture Organization study concluding that there has been for the whole world a 14 per cent increase in per capita food output since the prewar period.[1] At first glance, this would seem to indicate an improved future for the world's hungry people.

[1] *State of Food and Agriculture 1962* (Rome: The Food and Agriculture Organization), p. 16.

When we examine the picture more closely, however, we find serious problems. Table 2 shows that per capita food output in Latin America, Asia, and Africa is no better than it was twenty-five years ago—progress has occurred almost exclusively in North America, Western Europe, and the Soviet Union, even though the picture brightened for Latin America and for non-Communist Asia during the 1950's.

TABLE 2. Food: Per Capita Production by World Areas, Prewar to 1960
(Indexes: 1952–53 to 1956–57 = 100)

	Prewar	1948–49 to 1952–53	1960–61
World (excluding mainland China)	94	94	107
Northern America	85	99	100
U.S.	86	100	101
Latin America	103	97	101
Mexico	91		125
Brazil	109		109
Argentina	113		89
Western Europe	93	89	113
U.K.	76		112
France	88		118
Italy	87		105
East Europe & USSR	85	92	123
Non-Communist Asia [1]	106	93	106
India	} 107		105
Pakistan			102
Indonesia	117		96
Japan	102		118
Africa	97	98	98
Egypt (U.A.R.)	99		108
Algeria			116
Oceania	108	102	106
Australia	112		108

[1] Far East, excluding mainland China.
Source: FAO, *State of Food and Agriculture 1962*, pp. 14, 165, 166; *1963*, pp. 181–82.

Moreover, the areas which have lagged contain two-thirds of the world's population, and have notoriously poor diets. The lag seems to be due partly to rapid rates of population growth, and partly to failure of these areas (except perhaps Mexico and Japan) to participate sufficiently in the agricultural revolution that has brought such large increases in output per man and per acre in North America and Western Europe.

The rate of increase is only part of the picture, and should be complemented by data on levels of consumption. Table 3 gives rough and partial data on consumption of calories, the most commonly used single measure of diet. It will be noted that the well-fed areas, like the United States and Western Europe, consume about 50 per cent more per capita than do the poorest areas. This difference means partial starvation for a majority of the poorer areas of the world, but it is not a large gap relative to the possibilities of increased production. However, differences much greater than 50 per cent occur in the consumption of such vital but expensive food elements as proteins and vitamins, for which consumption figures in the richer countries run several times those in the poorer.

As one means of combining these divergent measures of diet, Figure 6 is reproduced from an FAO study. This chart portrays the diet in different areas in terms of their values, that is, the sums of the price-weighted farm commodities used for food. This way of looking at food facts gives the Far East a diet about one-sixth as valuable as that in North America (indexes of about 51 and 312, respectively, where 100 equals the world average for the years 1948–52). Western Europe, which on a calorie basis is 94 per cent as well off as North America, is by this "value" comparison only about 60 per cent as well off. As can be seen by the shaded

TABLE 3. Food: Calorie Consumption Per Capita by World Areas, Prewar to 1960–61

(calories available per day)

	1934–38	1948–49 to 1950–51	1960–61
World			2400e
Northern America	3200e	3170e	3120e
U.S.	3220	3180	3120
Latin America	2200?	2300e	2500
Mexico	...	...	2490[4]
Brazil	...	2180	2690[4]
Argentina	2730	3110[1]	2930[4]
Western Europe	2840	2750	2950
U.K.	3110	3130	3290[5]
France	2870	2800	2990[5]
Italy	2520	2350	2740
East Europe & USSR	2200?	...	2900a
USSR	...	...	2900a
China, Communist Asia	...	...	2100a
Non-Communist Asia	2000?	1800?	2100a
India	1970	1700[2]	2040
Pakistan		2010[2]	1970
Indonesia	...	...	2100a[6]
Japan	2180	1900	2240
Africa	2300?	2400?	2400a
Egypt (U.A.R.)	2450	2370	2530
So. Rhodesia	...	2150[3]	...
Oceania	3250e	3200e	3100e
Australia	3300	3220	3150

[1] 1951
[2] 1949/50–1950/51
[3] 1951–53
[4] 1960
[5] 1959/60
[6] 1958

e - rough estimate by authors.
? - guess by authors.
... - data unavailable.
a - estimate based on U.S. Dept. of Agriculture, *Food Balance in Foreign Countries* (for 1958) and *The World Food Budget 1962 and 1966*, p. 15.

Source: FAO, *Yearbook of Food and Agricultural Statistics*, Part I, 1956, 1961, 1962.
FAO, *State of Food and Agriculture*, various years.

FIGURE 6. Estimated Values of Food Supplies Per Capita by World Regions, Prewar to 1958–60

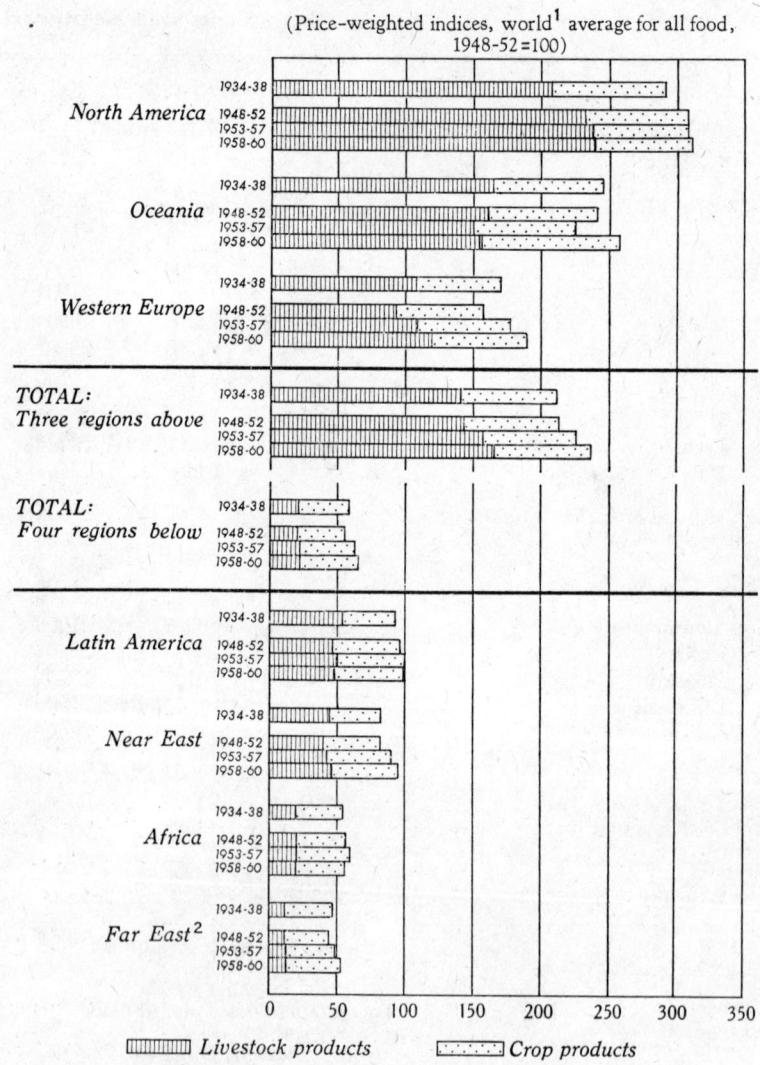

1. Excluding U.S.S.R., eastern Europe and Mainland China.
2. Excluding Mainland China.

Source: **Food and Agriculture Organization,** *State of Food and Agriculture 1961* (Rome: The Food and Agriculture Organization), p. 30.

portions of the bars in the chart, most of the differences arise in the values of livestock products (meat, milk, eggs, etc.) consumed. Large increases in the proteins supplied by such products are required for an adequate diet in the underdeveloped parts of the world, even though minimum nutritional standards can be met by a level of consumption well below the average for North America.

To summarize the food output picture, the past twenty-five years have shown a moderate improvement but there is still a long way to go, and progress is least where it is needed the most.

Energy. The second most important of the available indexes of materials supply is that for energy. The United Nations has estimated a total of all mineral and hydroelectric energy consumption annually since 1929 in terms of coal equivalents per capita, as presented in Table 4.

The rates of growth depicted here are much more encouraging than those for food shown in Table 2. Not only do the trends of the past twenty-five years incline more steeply upward (1¾ per cent per year instead of ½ per cent per year), but growth seems generally greater in areas where consumption is lowest. Thus Western Europe and the United States show increases of only 19 per cent and 36 per cent for 1937–60 while non-Communist Asia shows 39 per cent, Africa over 100 per cent, and Latin America and the Soviet Union show over 150 per cent increases in this period. It is well to note, however, that the range of disparities in energy consumption among different countries are of the order of 100-to-1, whereas in food values they are only of the order of 6-to-1 (Figure 6) and in calories less than 2-to-1 (Table 3).

For energy the picture is clearly brightening. Per capita consumption of energy is increasing rapidly, with the in-

TABLE 4. Energy: Per Capita Consumption by World Areas, 1929 to 1960

(kilograms of coal equivalent per year)

	1929	1937	1950	1960
World	867	900	1054	1405
Northern America	6400	5750e	7600e	7802
U.S.	6570	5890	7740	8013
Latin America	250e	260e	380e	670e
Mexico	300	440	600	1012
Brazil	100	130	220	372
Argentina	680	650	760	1069
Western Europe		2220e	2180e	2670e
U.K.	4110	4280	4420	4920
France	2420	2120	2030	2402
Italy	610	660	630	1186
East Europe & USSR		1100e		2720
USSR	420e	1000e	2000e	2847
China, Communist Asia		70	70e	600
Non-Communist Asia		180	170	250
India	70	90	100	140
Pakistan			40	67
Indonesia	50	50	60	134
Japan	740	930	780	1164
Africa	110	150	210	270
Egypt	150	130	220	281
Nigeria	20	20	40	39
Oceania	1800e	2140e	2600e	2947
Australia	1860	2270	3120	3902

e - rough estimate by the authors.

Sources: U.N., *World Energy Supplies in Selected Years 1929-1950; Statistical Yearbooks 1952, 1953, 1959, 1961,* and others.

Note: The U.N. data transcribed here are not wholly consistent over time. The ratios for conversion of hydropower to coal are subject to particular difficulties, and were lowered 86% between 1929 and 1960, reducing the 1960 world energy consumption by nearly 12% as compared to the aggregate which would have been computed by continued use of the 1929 ratio. However, the efficiency of conversion of coal to electricity has increased greatly in this 31-year period, so there is some justification for much of this change in the conversion ratio. If a single conversion ratio were used throughout, the growth in energy use would be larger.

There are also difficulties in determining the precise ratios of energy content as between the various mineral fuels, in estimating missing data, and in securing a consistent grouping of countries during the war and postwar changes. The data are therefore only approximate.

crease tending to concentrate in the poorer areas; but the distance to the standards of the advanced countries is still very great.

Nonfuel minerals. Variations in rates of growth for nonfuel minerals have been wide among countries. The increase in world output[2] of iron ore during the 1950's was nearly 100 per cent, with rates of increase in some of the less developed areas, such as Latin America and non-Communist Asia, running to several hundred per cent (Table 5). Western Europe and the Soviet Union also posted remarkable increases. It is well to note, however, that the big increases of the 1950's followed a war and postwar period in which the rate of increase was quite low—about 15 per cent per decade. For the period 1937–60 taken as a whole, the increase was about 45 per cent per decade. For comparison, the world's population increased 16 per cent per decade during this period.

For copper, the rate of growth in the 1950's was more moderate, averaging only 60 per cent for the world as a whole. The largest increases occurred in Australia, the Philippines, Rhodesia, Congo, Japan, Peru, and Chile. (See Table 6.)

For all metals taken together, the world price-weighted index of output rose about 72 per cent from 1938 to 1960.

---

[2] The remainder of this section covers only output, because the U.N. data do not include consumption. Aggregate figures are given instead of per capita, because outputs of most minerals have very little relation to population, or to the welfare of the population, since foreign trade constitutes such a large percentage of output and consumption for many countries. Thus in 1960 Venezuela produced 1.7 metric tons of iron per capita, the United Kingdom only .09 tons; Latin America produced over 8 pounds of copper per capita, Western Europe a little over ½ pound. Approximate calculations can be made with the data on population in Table 11; for world totals there is little difference between output and consumption in most years.

TABLE 5. Iron Ore: Total Output by World Areas, 1937 to 1960

(million metric tons Fe content)

	1937	1950	1960
World [1]	97.8[2]	116.9	231.1
Northern America	37.8	51.1	58.6
U.S.	37.0	49.3	47.9
Latin America	1.3	3.5	26.6
Brazil	0.1	1.4	6.4
Chile	0.9	1.8	3.8
Peru	—	—	3.1
Venezuela	...	0.1	12.5
Western Europe	33e	28.6	52.0
U.K.	4.3	4.0	4.7
France	11.5	9.7	21.7
Germany	2.8	2.8	4.6
Sweden	9.1	8.3	13.0
East Europe & USSR	18e	24.5	65.3
USSR	16.1	23.0	61.8
China, Communist Asia	...	...	27[3]
Non-Communist Asia	3.7	3.4	16.1
India	1.9	1.9	6.5
Malaya	1.0	0.3	3.2
Japan	0.3	0.5	1.6
Africa	3.4	4.0	9.2
Algeria	1.3	1.4	1.8
Liberia	—	—	2.1
South Africa	0.3	0.7	2.0
Oceania	1.3e	1.4e	3.0
Australia	1.3	1.4	2.9

[1] Excluding China.
[2] 1938 total was 74.9.
[3] Source, U.S. Bureau of Mines, *Minerals Yearbook 1961*, I:668.

e - rough estimate by the authors.
— - zero output.
... - data unavailable.

Sources: U.N. *Statistical Yearbook 1962* and *1957*.

TABLE 6. Copper Output by World Areas, 1937 to 1960

(1,000 metric tons of Cu in ore)

	1937	1950	1960
World [1]	2190	2270	3640
Northern America	1013	1065	1378
U.S.	764	825	980
Latin America	510	481	795
Mexico	46	62	60
Peru	36	30	182
Chile	413	363	536
Western Europe	74	57	90
Norway	21	16	15
Sweden	7	16	18
Finland	14	17	31
East Europe and USSR	...	...	...
East Germany	29	8	24
Yugoslavia	42	43	33
Non-Communist Asia	107	86	203
India	7	9	9
Philippines	2	10	44
Cyprus	28	16	32
Japan	67	39	89
Turkey	1	12	26
Africa	423	502	967
Congo	151	176	302
Rhodesia	250	281	581
South Africa	11	33	46
Oceania	...	...	...
Australia	20	18	111

[1] Total of areas reported. Omits China, U.S.S.R. and others.   ... - data unavailable.

Sources: U.N., *Statistical Yearbook 1962, 1958,* and others.

Output of some metals rose slowly, or even declined. Lead output rose 15 per cent from 1938 to 1960; zinc rose 50 per cent; tin declined 3 per cent; gold rose 5 per cent; silver declined 15 per cent (gold and silver data omit the Soviet Union). In contrast are bauxite, whose output rose 550 per cent during the twenty-two years, and the ferroalloy metals. Manganese output rose 120 per cent; nickel 150 per cent; chrome 220 per cent.

For a few significant nonfuel nonmetals, the increases in output for this same period (1938–1960) were: native sulfur, 130 per cent; phosphate rock, 210 per cent; potash, 205 per cent.

Forest products. Wood output increased about 40 per cent between 1946 (the earliest year for which the FAO presents a table covering most of the world) and 1960. (See Table 7.) This is at the rate of 25 per cent per decade, or $2\frac{1}{4}$ per cent per year, substantially more than the increase in population over this period. Largest increases appear to have occurred in Asia and Africa, and probably the Soviet Union; increases in Northern America, Latin America, and Western Europe were only 15 to 30 per cent in 1946–60.

The moderate change in the total conceals a substantial increase in the removals of lumber-grade materials, a very large increase in pulpwood and pitprops, and a quite small rise in output of fuelwood, which rose less than population.

EMPLOYMENT/OUTPUT RATIO

Our second index for indicating scarcity is trends in the productivity of labor. United Nations data are summarized in Table 8. The agricultural data, though sketchy, look quite encouraging. While they reflect the strong upsurge

TABLE 7. Total Wood Removals by World Areas, 1946 to 1960

(roundwood—mil. cu. meters)

	1946	1953	1960
World	1300e	1470[4]	1794[4]
Northern America	356	367	405
U.S.	272	279	309
Latin America	140e	158	188[4]
Mexico	3.9	3.7	12e
Brazil	109.6	94.9[5]	102.1[5,6]
Argentina	15e	15.3	12.1
Western Europe	200e	184	249[4]
Germany	44.4	22.4	25.3
France	24.4	33.7	41.2
Finland	29.9[5]	31.0[5]	48.1
Italy	16.4	12.8	17.3
Sweden	38.5	34.7	46.0
East Europe and USSR	250?	355	437
USSR	200?	292[4]	370
China, Communist Asia	40?	50e	70e
Non-Communist Asia	150e	200e	230e
India	...	14.6	15.6[1]
Indonesia	50e	70e	80.7
Japan	43.4	52.5	69.4
Africa	100e	160e	184[4]
Tanganyika	...	10e	10.8
Sudan	0.4[2]	13.0	14.0
Uganda	0.4[3]	10.4	10.7
Oceania[7]	15.3	21.9	25.2[4]
Australia	12.4	18.0	15.8

[1] 1957
[2] 1947; incomplete data.
[3] 1947
[4] From Summary Table, 1962 *Yearbook*, (see source below).
[5] Understatement ("incomplete total").
[6] 1958
[7] Listed as "Pacific Area," but constituent islands appear to be same.
e - rough estimate or extrapolation by authors.
? - guess by the authors.
... - data unavailable.

Sources: FAO, *Yearbook of Forest Products Statistics, 1948, 1949, 1955, 1962*, Table 1.

in productivity in North America and West Europe from the impact of the agricultural revolution which has occurred in the past twenty-five years, declines in labor required per unit of output also appear to be substantial in Latin America and Asia. It is, however, necessary to warn that the agricultural data are particularly liable to error. Censuses of farm labor are subject to error because of doubt as to how much child and female labor to count, and because standards of counting change from one census to another. It is also difficult to find output data for the same years for which labor input data are available. Attention should also be called to the fact that in Table 8 the early and late years compared by the agricultural indexes are not the same for all the countries reported.

The last two columns in Table 8 show the decline in mining labor per unit of output. It will be noted that labor required per unit of output for the world as a whole declined 29 per cent on the average between 1938 and 1953. The six national indexes we have been able to estimate for 1960 or thereabouts indicate considerable further progress since 1953.

In summary, the productivity data show an improving trend in the raw materials industries, which should support rising levels of living. The more productivity can be increased (which would be reflected in a lowering of the employment/output ratio), the more rapidly living levels will rise.

RELATIVE PRICE TRENDS

Relative prices are our third indicator of scarcity trends. It is difficult to find series that are not seriously impaired by

TABLE 8. Changes in Employment/Output Ratios for Agriculture and Mining

	AGRICULTURE			MINING	
	Base year(s) (employment data/output data)	Recent year	Index Recent yr./ base yr. Base yr. = 100	Index 1938 = 100	
				1953	1960
World			...	71	...
Northern America			...	63	...
U.S. [1]	1934–38	1957	43	61	54
Latin America				48	...
Mexico	1940/prewar[2]	1958	60	108[3]	...
Brazil	1940/prewar[2]	1950	86	71[4]	41[5]
Argentina			...	160[6]	...
Western Europe			...	92	...
U.K.	1931/prewar[2]	1951	73	104[7]	109[8]
France	1936/prewar[2]	1957	57	93	64
Italy	1936/prewar[2]	1960	51	86[9]	29[10]
Non-Communist Asia			...	92	...
India	1931/prewar[2]	1951	80e	...	...
Japan	1930/prewar[2]	1959	89	106[11]	96
Oceania			...	59	...
Australia	1933/prewar[2]	1954	75	...	...

e - rough estimate by the authors.
... - not available.
[1] From Potter and Christy, *op. cit.*, pp. 236 and 501–2.
[2] "Prewar" designates a period such as 1934–38. The first date in this column indicates the year for which the employment or occupational count was given. It will be clear, therefore, that the employment and output data are not for the same period of time, and that the indexes in the third column are only crude approximations.
[3] 1955/39. The employment data appear to include nonferrous metallurgy and petroleum refining.
[4] 1953 related to 1939 employment and 1938 output.
[5] 1958 related to 1939 employment and 1938 output.
[6] 1954/1939
[7] 1953 related to 1935 employment and 1938 output.
[8] 1958 related to 1935 employment and 1938 output.
[9] 1951/1938
[10] 1961/1938
[11] 1954/1938, with a rough adjustment for discontinuity in series.

Sources: U.N. Food and Agriculture Organization, *Production Yearbooks,* 1961 and 1957. U.N., *Statistical Yearbooks, 1962,* Tables 12 and 39; *1959,* Tables 13 and 39; *1956,* Table 37; and others. U.N., *Patterns of Industrial Growth, 1938–1958.*

changing value standards, fluctuating exchange rates, and artificially fixed or supported prices. However, a few series are available which appear to be reasonably good indicators; they relate chiefly to standard commodities which have been traded on a fairly free world market over the past fifty years or so. In Table 9 we show four of these, deflated by the U.S. general wholesale price index (adjusted where necessary for changes in the rate of exchange between the dollar and the British pound) so as to register the prices in a more-or-less constant monetary unit. The constant dollar price of sugar has fallen by about one-half since the pre-World War I period (1900–10 in Table 9); wheat has fallen over 25 per cent, cotton about 20 per cent, and copper 25 to 40 per cent.

The last column of Table 9 shows a U.N. worldwide index of the export prices of food and raw materials, deflated by the export price of manufactured goods. The broad coverage is an advantage as compared to statistics on individual commodities presented in the first four columns, but the short time span leaves us with less sense of a trend, particularly because there were such drastic upheavals in price levels during the 1938–1960 period, and price controls were quite prevalent. The comprehensive index does, however, move reasonably parallel to the single-commodity series over the period for which it is available. Incomplete as it is, the picture obtained from looking at these few price series is not one of increasing scarcity; quite the opposite is indicated.

NET IMPORT TRENDS

Fourth, let us take a look at the growth of trade in raw materials as an indicator of scarcity, not from the viewpoint

World Trends in Resources

TABLE 9. Indexes of World Prices of Selected Resource Commodities, 1900 to 1960

(deflated as indicated)

	Wheat[1]	Sugar[2]	Cotton[3]	Copper[4]	World index of materials export prices[5]
1900	238	9.3	23.7	980	
1905	251	8.8	28.1	865	
1910	234	7.3	32.0	607	
1915	387	9.3	25.8	781	
1920	222	13.3	16.5	473	
1925	260	4.5	29.3	448	
1929	208	3.8	26.1	593	
1930	143	3.1	18.0	474	
1934	160	2.2	25.5	314	
1935	187	2.3	22.4	301	
1936	261	2.3	24.4	364	
1937	234	2.8	15.7	480	
1938	159	2.7	17.1	390	68
1947	306	7.1	35.7	546	...
1948	343	5.6	30.6	517	100
1949	300	5.8	31.9	495	...
1950	234	6.7	41.0	483	115
1951	218	6.9	34.3	497	116
1952	237	5.2	30.8	651	101
1953	244	4.3	30.2	647	100
1954	209	4.1	30.6	632	101
1955	201	4.1	26.7	890	100
1956	185	4.2	22.4	806	96
1957	182	6.1	22.1	523	96
1958	177	4.1	21.3	465	89
1959	176	3.4	19.9	557	86
1960	175	3.6	21.2	576	83

... – data unavailable.

[1] Liverpool: cents/bushel, deflated by U.S. general wholesale price index, 1947–49 = 100.

[2] Raw sugar: cents/lb., deflated by U.S. general wholesale price index, 1957 = 100; c.i.f. New York for 1900–31; f.a.s. Cuban basis, 1932–59, linked to New York series at 1931. Source: FAO, *The World Sugar Economy in Figures, 1880–1959* (Rome, FAO, no date), p. 127; FAO, *Production Yearbook, 1961*, p. 303, "Cuba: I" price.

[3] Texas, cents/lb., ⅞ inch to 1 inch, at Liverpool and at New Orleans, deflated by U.S. general wholesale price index, 1947–49 = 100.

[4] London, annual average price per ton of G.M.B. and Standard copper, converted to dollars at annual average exchange rates and deflated by general wholesale price index (1947–49 = 100).

[5] U.N. export price index for foods and raw materials deflated by export prices of manufactured goods; 1953 = 100. (U.N. *Statistical Yearbook 1961*, p. 426 for 1938, 1948, and 1952–60; *1959* for 1950 and 1951.)

Sources: FAO, U.S. Dept. of Agriculture, *Metal Statistics*, and others.

of the whole world, of course, but from the viewpoint of particular areas. The FAO indexes (Table 10) show a 41 per cent increase in total world imports of food and feedstuffs since the prewar period, and an increase of over 50 per cent in the past ten years. The biggest changes came in the shift of North America from a small net import balance, due largely to the droughts of the 1930's, to large net exports, and the shift of the Near East and Asia from small net exports to large net imports.

In breadgrains, principally wheat and rye, little change took place in the balance of trade between 1934–38 and 1960 for Europe, the Soviet Union, or Oceania. But North America increased its exports very heavily (in 1960 U.S. net exports of these grains were 47 per cent of output), while Asia imported half the increased exports, and South America and Africa absorbed small amounts. In feed grains (corn, barley, oats, and sorghum) Europe has absorbed a good portion of the increased exports, while Asia, being still very poor, has imported little, for keeping livestock is a relatively expensive business. Latin America has reduced its exports over one-half.

The 150 per cent increase in imports of food and feedstuffs by the non-Communist Far East in the decade of the 1950's reflects a growth in dependency on outside resources, though it is still below the absolute levels of Europe's imports, as indicated by parts (2) and (3) of Table 10. The rate of increase in the Near East is also striking, though the absolute amounts here are considerably smaller than for Asia.

Do these growing imports reflect increasing scarcity of agricultural resources in these countries? The answer cannot be clear-cut because the recent growth in imports has been in large part a result of increased availability of mone-

TABLE 10. Net Imports, Food and Feed

	(1) All food & feedstuffs (1952-53 =100)		
	1934-38	1948-52	1960
World (gross imports)	100	92	141
Northern America	+	−95	−162
Latin America	−178	−122	−179
Western Europe	125	106	130
Far East except mainland China	—	61	147
Near East	—	115	532
Africa	−94	−94	−85
Oceania	−87	−95	−115

	(2) Breadgrains			(3) Feedgrains			(4) Oilseeds & oils (oil equivalents)		
	1934-38	1948-52	1960	1934-38	1948-52	1960	1934-38	1948-52	1960
	\- - - - - millions of metric tons - - - - -								
World (gross imports)	10	20.1	22.9a	9.8	8.1	15.8	3.49	2.46	3.27
Northern America	−4.8	−17.3	−23.8	−0.1	−4.6	−11.4	.93	.14	−1.01
Latin America	−2.3	−0.3	(−0.8)	−7.4	−1.7	−3.3	−.58	−.28	−.22
Asia	0.9	5.1	10.4	−1.0	0.7	1.3	−1.07	−1.89	−.56
Europe	9.5	13.9	8.7	9.8	7.4	14.5	2.56	2.31	3.26
USSR	−1.0	...	...	−0.4	...	...	0	.005	.005
Africa	−0.1	1.1	3.0	−0.8	−0.7	−1.0	−.91	−1.06	−1.35
Oceania	−2.7	−2.9	−3.4	−0.1	−0.5	−0.6	−.10	−.08	−.11

+ = net imports, − = net exports, ... = data unavailable.
A "+" or a "−" alone in a column indicates that the net imports (or net exports, as the case may be) of the region in question were of opposite direction (or algebraic sign) from those in the base period. It is considered inappropriate to compute an index number on a base of opposite sign.
a The sizeable difference between total world imports and the sum of exports in the rest of the column appears to be due to differences in times and methods of recording shipment by exporting and importing countries.

Sources: FAO, State of Food and Agriculture, 1962, pp. 42, 193.
FAO, Trade Yearbook 1961, pp. 107, 255.

tary exchange from the U.S. foreign aid program and oil exports from the Near East, and the subsidies given to agricultural exports by the United States. For Europe, the heaviest importer of foods and feedstuffs, present absolute levels of imports are about the same as prewar, reflecting a considerable per capita reduction of imports.

Trade in other raw materials is considerably smaller than that in agricultural products. In 1960 world food and "raw materials"[3] imports totalled $39.5 billion. The next largest group of resource materials was fuels, totalling $10.8 bil-

---

[3] Presumably fabrication materials, including textile fibers, construction materials, woodpulp, metal ores, etc.

lion.[4] However, while the values are smaller, the rate of increase in international fuel trade is more steeply upward than that for food and raw materials: the 1960 quantity of fuel traded was 170 per cent above 1938 and 80 per cent above 1950.[5]

As noteworthy as the sharp rate of growth in the fuels trade, is the fact that a number of nations are almost wholly dependent on imports for their energy supplies, while other nations are thoroughly dependent on exports for their national prosperity. In 1960, Italy, for example, produced only 31 per cent of its energy needs, Sweden 16 per cent, and the Philippines 7 per cent. Venezuela's 1960 exports were 90 per cent petroleum and products; Iraq's 97 per cent; for Iran the figure was 74 per cent in 1958.

Net imports as an indication of resource scarcity, therefore, present a variety of pictures, country by country, but generally of increasing dependence on sources or markets in other countries. For the world as a whole increasing dependence, or linkage, among the countries for their raw materials should work in the direction of lower costs generally speaking and, therefore, increases in living levels, as fuller advantage is taken of more favorable international locations of resources.

CONCLUSION

It has not been possible to assemble historical data on resource trends in the other world areas as systematically or comprehensively as was done for the United States in Chapter 2. Although the foregoing effort to examine such evi-

[4] U.N. *Statistical Yearbook 1961*, p. 426.
[5] U.N. *Statistical Yearbook 1961*, p. 426; and *1959*, p. 405.

dence as could be brought readily to hand is far from conclusive, it does warn against easy generalizations that the rest of the world is about to run out of raw materials or, conversely, that the less developed areas are going to take off right away into rapid improvements in living levels because of plentiful supplies of food, energy, and raw materials. The picture is mixed: quite favorable for energy commodities, much less so for food. For some less developed but heavily populated countries the race between food and people apparently will be a close one. As with the United States, only more dramatically, much will depend on the rate at which technological advances already proven can be broadly applied, and on keeping open the channels of world trade. One hopes that data on resource commodity trends can be improved as time goes on; if so, our scarcity indicators can be improved as guides for policies and actions.

CHAPTER

4

Projections of
Resource Demands

Let us now take a look at levels of demand for resources and raw materials which would arise by the year 2000 under a few simple assumptions. Taking the high population projections of the United Nations' 1958 study as shown in Table 11,[1] we have made rough estimates of the materials which would be consumed in the year 2000 under each of the following assumptions:

[1] The figures for 1980 and 2000 given in Table 11 are the "high" projections of the United Nations' *Future Growth of World Population* (1958). Demographers in more recent projections seem to agree that this projection is indicated as more likely to approximate the events of the future than the medium or low projections, which aggregate 6,280 million and 4,880 million for the year 2000 population of the world. Furthermore, use of the "high" estimates has the advantage of revealing possible resource shortages sooner and more clearly. See, for example, Frank W. Notestein's "guess" of 6,919 million for the year 2000, in "World Population Trends," a contribution to the *World Food Forum*, U.S. Dept. of Agriculture, May 1962; and Harold F. Dorn's use of U.N. high projections at the Twenty-third American Assembly in a paper published in *The Population Dilemma*, Philip M. Hauser, editor, Prentice-Hall, Inc., 1963.

The high projection for world population in 2000 is about 10 per cent above the medium projection, and this provides a rough and ready basis for conversion to the medium level.

We would note that in thus casually taking a population projection for the year 2000, we make no assumption that that *will* be the population, for this depends on a multitude of social attitudes and adjustments relative to birth rates and the availability of resources, among many factors. Our purpose is simply to set up a reasonably high target and then to examine the difficulties which resource scarcities may pose in reaching it.

1. The trends in resource consumption during the decade of the 1950's continue for the next four decades in the several parts of the world.

2. The average per capita level of consumption for the world as a whole in the year 2000 is at the level attained in the United States in 1960.[2]

3. The average level of consumption in the world is at the level attained by Western Europe in 1960.

4. The United States, Europe, the Soviet Union, and Oceania consume at the rate of the United States in 1960, while the rest of the world attains the level of Western Europe in 1960.

FOOD PRODUCTS

Applying each of the four assumptions in turn to the available data on food[3] results in the following projected increases:

---

[2] This appears to omit an allowance for rising standards in the United States, but in terms of world totals the omission is not large, since U.S. population is projected at only 4¼ per cent of the world total and increases in per capita consumption of raw materials in the United States recently have been only about ⅓ per cent a year.

[3] These projections are less sophisticated than a number of others available for the interested reader. One we would mention is that of Egbert de Vries, Rector, Netherlands Institute of Social Studies, published in *World Food Forum Proceedings* commemorating the centennial of U.S. Department of Agriculture (Washington, January, 1963). With considerably more detailed tables than those given here, de Vries indicates the need for concern over the growing imbalance between food output and consumption in Asia, and the lag in outputs in South America and Africa.

In another paper in the same book, Willard W. Cochrane, then Director of Agricultural Economics in the U.S. Department of Agriculture, foresees even greater deficits in food for the underdeveloped countries, and points out their impact in severely limiting economic development, as hungry populations cause shortages of foreign exchange and savings.

TABLE 11. Population Trends: Historical 1920–1960, and Projections 1980 and 2000, by World Areas

(millions)

	1920	1938	1950	1960	1980 (U.N. high projections)	2000
World	1811	2170[1]	2510	2995	4280	6900
Northern America	117	143	167	199	255	326
U.S.	106	130	152	181	230e	293e
Canada	8.8	11.4	13.7	17.8	25e	32e
Latin America	91	125e	162	206	349	651
Mexico	...	19.1	25.8	35.0	61e	
Brazil	27.4	39.5	52.0	70.8	116e	
Argentina	8.9	13.7	17.2	20.0	29e	
Western Europe	246e	265e	286	307	360e	430e
U.K.	43.7	47.7e	50.6	52.5	58e	
France	39.0	41.4e	41.7	45.5	51e	
Italy	37.0	43.1e	46.6	49.4	59e	
W. Germany (inc. W. Berlin)	37e	42e	50.0	55.6	67e	
East Europe & USSR	250e	290e	279e	332	440e	560e
USSR	158	188e	181	214	297	395
Poland	...	...	24.8	29.7	36e	
China, Communist Asia	430e	490e	590e	710e	1050e	1800e
Non-Communist Asia	500e	680e	790e	970	1430e	2500e
Turkey	12e	17.2	20.9	27.8	45e	
India	} 250	308	358	433	650e	
Pakistan		69	75	93	144e	
Indonesia	52	68	76	93	137e	
Philippines	10e	16	20	27.8	50e	
Japan	55	70	83	93	124	
Africa	141	169	206	254	375	663
Algeria	...	...	8.8	11.0	17e	
Egypt	13.2	16.4	20.4	25.9	43e	
Nigeria	...	...	24.3	35.1	50e	
South Africa	6.8	10.0	12.4	15.8	26e	
Congo	6.7e	10.3	11.3	14.1	19e	
Oceania	8.8	11.0e	13.0	16.5	22	30
Australia	5.4	6.9	8.2	10.3	14e	18e

[1] 1937   ... = data unavailable.

e - rough estimates by the authors. The U.S. figures for 1980 and 2000 were calculated so as to be consistent with the U.N. estimate for all Northern America; consequently they are lower than the figures used in Resources for the Future's 1963 study, *Resources in America's Future* (245 million for 1980 and 331 million for 2000).

Sources: U.N. *Demographic Yearbook*, 1956, 1961; U.N. *The Future Growth of World Population* (Population Studies, No. 28, 1958); U.N., *Statistical Yearbook*, 1957, 1961; and others; plus estimates of the authors, involving adjustments or extrapolations of U.N. data.

Projections of Resource Demands

1. The indexes of FAO show an increase in world per capita food consumption of 8 per cent between the average for 1948–52 and that for 1957–59. In four decades, this rate of increase would compound to 47 per cent, to which must be added the increase due to the more than doubling of world population.
2. To raise the average calorie consumption of the world by the year 2000 to the level attained by the United States in 1960 would involve a 30 per cent increase per capita. The increase in proteins and other food elements would be much larger, but we shall discuss this later.
3. The increase in average world consumption of calories to attain a West European 1960 level would be 23 per cent per capita.
4. If Northern America, Europe, the Soviet Union, and Oceania consumed at the U.S. 1960 levels, and the rest of the world consumed at West European 1960 levels, world per capita calorie intake would be 24 per cent above its actual 1960 level.

Table 12 summarizes the number of calories that would be consumed under each of the above assumptions. This is done by combining the projected changes in per capita consumption with the population projections of Table 11. Thus in column (1), for the world, per capita consumption in 2000 would be 47 per cent above the 1960 levels and population 130 per cent over 1960. Combined, these percentages give an increase of 240 per cent. The 7,200 billion 1960 world total calorie intake, increased by 240 per cent, is the 24,000 billion calories shown in column (1) for the world.

It is most interesting that the consumption trends of the 1950's should give us a projection for year 2000 which is

TABLE 12. Projections of Calorie Consumption in the Year 2000 Compared to 1960 Actual for World Areas

(billions per day)

	1960 actual	Trend of 1948–52 to 1957–59 continues (1)	World is at U.S. 1960 per capita level of consumption (2)	World is at West Europe 1960 per capita level (3)	N. Am., Europe, USSR, and Oceania at U.S. 1960 per capita level; rest at Europe 1960 level (4)
World	7,200	24,000	21,500	20,400	20,600
Northern America	620	900	1,020	960	1,020
Latin America	520	2,500	2,000	1,900	1,900
Western Europe	910	{4,700}	1,340	1,270	1,340
East Europe and USSR	960e		1,700	1,650	1,700
Communist Asia	1,500e	{13,800}	5,600	5,300	5,300
Non-Communist Asia	2,000e		7,800	7,400	7,400
Africa	600e	1,600[1]	2,100	1,950	1,950
Oceania	53	100	90	90	90

e - rough estimate by the authors.

[1] Extrapolating trend in per capita production in 1948–52 to 1957–59, for lack of consumption data. *Source*: FAO, *Third World Food Survey*, Appendix Table 3A.

Source: 1960 actual: Population data of Table 11 multiplied by consumption estimates of Table 3.
  Col. (1): FAO, *Third World Food Survey* (Rome, 1963), Table 13.
  Col. (2): Population projections of Table 11 multiplied by U.S. per capita consumption in 1960/61 (Table 3: 3120 calories).
  Col. (3): Same population, multiplied by 1960/61 consumption in Western Europe (Table 3: 2950 calories).
  Col. (4): Same population, multiplied by U.S. and Western Europe 1960/61 consumption levels, as indicated in column heading.

higher than any of the three consumption "goals" set forth in assumptions 2, 3, and 4. This does not mean, however, that an adequate diet is fast approaching for the world's hungry people, because:

Projections of Resource Demands

1. Continuation of the recent trend for some areas would carry them past the point of satiation by the year 2000. Note, for example, that column (1) is higher than column (2) for Latin America and Europe. Clearly, these areas in 2000 will not consume calories at a per capita rate higher than Northern America in 1960. Thus our total of 24,000 billion contains some over-inflated figures; we can be sure trends will change, and the result will be a lower total than shown in column (1).

2. There are doubts as to the accuracy of the estimates for the U.S.S.R. and mainland China.

3. There may be great difficulties in maintaining for forty years the rate of increase in output achieved between 1948–52 and 1957–59, particularly because the 1950's included a significant amount of recovery from wartime damage and neglect in Europe, the Soviet Union, and Japan, as well as considerable impact from recent agricultural discoveries, such as DDT, 2,4–D, and hybrid corn.

4. There are much larger and more serious deficiencies in proteins and vitamins in the world's average diet. While the world needs only a 20 to 30 per cent increase in per capita calorie intake, it needs a 40 or 50 per cent increase in its total protein supply to reach West European standards of 1960. The increase in animal proteins (milk, eggs, meat, etc.) required would be of the order of 200–300 per cent.[4]

---

[4] *State of Food and Agriculture 1962* (Rome: The Food and Agriculture Organization), pp. 129ff.

ENERGY COMMODITIES

In Table 13 energy consumption for the year 2000 is projected on the basis of each of four assumptions given at the opening of the chapter. These assumptions and their implications for energy are as follows:

1. Per capita consumption in each continental area continues to increase at the rate at which it increased in the decade of 1950–60 [column (1) of Table 13]. This would result in an aggregate consumption in year 2000 a little over five times that of 1960. This assumption looks quite possible, since it is based on a rate of growth that has actually been experienced. It should be noted, however, that the decade of the 1950's was one of booming economies in most of the world, so this may be a higher rate of increase than can be sustained to the year 2000.[5] On the other hand national economies in stages of rapid industrial development may well require as much as a doubling of energy input each ten to twenty years.

2. That the world average consumption in the year 2000 would be as great as that of the United States in 1960 [Table 13, column (2)]. This is a very generous assumption, as U.S. per capita consumption in 1960 was nearly six times the world average and three times that of Western Europe. On this assumption, the total consumption in the year 2000 would be thirteen times that of 1960.

---

[5] The figure for Communist China is surprisingly high for the year 1960, giving a rate of increase for the decade that would be almost impossible to imagine for the next forty years; so we have used a rate of increase equal to that estimated for non-Communist Asia for this decade. The per capita consumption in the U.S.S.R. and East Europe has been limited at the U.S. year 2000 level, viz., 8,220 kg. coal equivalent per year.

3. That world average per capita consumption would equal that of Western Europe in 1960. This is a much more modest assumption, and gives a world total a little over four times that of 1960 [Table 13, column (3)].

4. That the United States, Europe, the U.S.S.R., and Oceania consume at the rate of the United States in the year 1960, while all the rest of the world consumes at the level attained by Western Europe in 1960. This gives a world total consumption six times that of 1960 [Table 13, column (4)].

TABLE 13. Projections of Energy Consumed in 2000 Compared to 1960 Actual by World Areas

(billions of metric tons of coal equivalent)

	1960 actual	Energy consumption in year 2000 if:			
		Trend in consumption from 1950 to 1960 continues (1)	World consumption is at U.S. 1960 per capita level (2)	World consumption is at W. Europe 1960 per capita level (3)	N. Am., Europe, USSR, and Oceania at U.S. 1960 per capita level; rest at Europe 1960 level (4)
World	4.2	22.4	55.3	17.7	25.1
Northern America	1.55	2.68	2.61	.84	2.61
Latin America	.14	3.18	5.22	1.67	1.67
Western Europe	.79	2.98	3.45	1.10	3.45
East Europe & USSR	.90	4.6?	4.49	1.44	4.49
Communist Asia	.40	5.0?	11.1	4.6	4.6
Non-Communist Asia	.24	2.9	20.0	6.4	6.4
Africa	.08	1.0	5.31	1.70	1.70
Oceania	.05	.10	.24	.08	.24

? - guess by the authors.
Source: See text above.

Taking these assumptions and projections together, it seems quite possible that the year 2000 world consumption of energy will be about five times that of 1960 or, to speak more realistically in terms of a range, four to six times as great. World consumption of energy in 2000 at the 1960 U.S. level appears unattainable, although rates of increase in other parts of the world, especially the less developed areas, are expected greatly to exceed that of the United States during the next forty years.[6]

NONFUEL MINERALS

Continuation for the next four decades of the phenomenal growth in world iron ore output which occurred in the 1950's (see Table 5) would produce a fourteen-fold increase, or a six-fold increase per capita. This is roughly the same as the U.S. rate of increase during its forty years of fastest growth in production of iron.[7] Despite its steepness, this may be a possible rate of growth for some parts of the world. However, it seems unlikely that the recent rates of growth in output for Latin America, the Soviet Union, and Asia can continue for forty years. Moreover, they would result in world consumption of nearly ½ ton per capita as compared to U.S. 1960 consumption of 1/3 ton, and Western Europe's per capita of 1/6 ton. Extrapolation of the 1937–60 rate of increase yields a five-fold increase in aggregate output by

---

[6] Assumption 1 gives increases in consumption in the underdeveloped areas of about ten-fold. The U.S. increase in consumption of mineral fuels in the period 1860–1900 was six-fold, starting from a level about that of the underdeveloped nations today. Sam H. Schurr et al., *Energy in the American Economy, 1850–1975* (Baltimore: The Johns Hopkins Press for Resources for the Future, 1960), p. 521.

[7] Potter and Christy, *Trends in Natural Resource Commodities* (Baltimore: The Johns Hopkins Press for Resources for the Future, 1962), pp. 37, 376.

the year 2000, and would provide a world per capita consumption of about 1/6 ton.

The growth in output projected for copper at the 1950–60 rate (see Table 6) would be modest compared to that of the United States during its "take-off" forty-year period—about six-fold compared to nearly forty-fold. Nevertheless, the fact that the older producing areas, like the United States, Chile, and Europe, show slower rates of growth, plus the fact that the 1937–60 growth was only 65 per cent (25 per cent per decade) suggest that even a six-fold increase may not be attained by the year 2000. Perhaps a three-fold increase is more likely; this would mean a world consumption of about $3\frac{1}{2}$ pounds per capita, as against 1960 consumptions of about 13 pounds by the United States and Western Europe, 7 pounds by Japan, and 5 pounds by Russia.[8] Aluminum is now available for important uses formerly met by copper.

A number of other significant minerals may be mentioned briefly. It appears that growth rates for ferroalloys may be about as high as for iron, while a much higher rate of growth for bauxite seems inevitable as use of aluminum continues to expand rapidly in construction, transportation equipment, and electrical goods. Other metals may experience a slower rate of growth than during the recent past. Such nonmetals as sulfur, phosphate, and potash may experience fairly high rates of growth—several hundred per cent over the forty years as fertilizer and other chemical industries grow.

---

[8] American Metal Market, *Metal Statistics 1960*, p. 289. U.S. consumption is primary only; others appear to include secondary copper (about 10 per cent of total in U.S.).

FOREST PRODUCTS

The increase in the rate of wood removals from the forests of the world between 1946 and 1960 was about 40 per cent (Table 7). Projected for the next forty years, this rate of increase would mean another 150 per cent increase in the annual cut. Even the 40 per cent rate of increase in aggregate cut in the past fourteen years has been moderated by the inclusion of fuelwood which increased very little. Sawlog cutting (for lumber and plywood) increased 66 per cent in the fourteen years 1946–60; projected for forty years this gives an increase of over 300 per cent (or 70 per cent per capita). In view of the downtrend in per capita consumption of sawlogs in the United States in the past fifty years, and the sharp rate of increase in prices, we feel no assurance that these world forest product projections will actually be experienced. However, the available lumber per capita, with a 70 per cent increase, would be less than half U.S. 1960 levels, though considerably above the levels of consumption in Western Europe in 1960.[9]

[9] *Yearbook of Forest Products Statistics 1962* (Rome: The Food and Agriculture Organization), p. 120.

Note to second printing, February, 1966: Publications issued since the above was written slightly modify the data, but offer no basis for essential modification of this report. New UN population estimates raise slightly the 1960 world total, raise the 1980 projection about 10%, and lower the year 2000 projection about 1% ("high" variants in each case). Changes for the different continents in the year 2000 are unimportant except for Africa (new estimate 30% higher), Northern America (up 15%), and Communist Asia (down 14%).

In the per capita production of food for the world, there has been no progress since 1959-60, though there were continued but irregular gains in the preceding decade. Preliminary estimates for the crop year 1963-64 indicate it was the fifth year in succession without significant change in world per capita agricultural production (FAO, *State of Food and Agriculture 1964*, p. 3). Per capita consumption of energy, however, continued its climb in nearly all areas (*UN Statistical Yearbook 1963*, pp. 313-15), while aggregate outputs of metal ores rose slightly more than population except for iron, which rose slightly less (*ibid.*, pp. 175-79).

CHAPTER

5

Reserves and Alternate Supply Possibilities

Will it be possible to increase the output of food, energy, wood products, minerals, and other raw materials so as to reach the levels projected in the preceding section? By the year 2000 this would involve roughly:

1. A tripling of aggregate food output, just to provide adequate calories, and considerably more to provide adequate proteins and vitamins.[1]
2. A five-fold increase in energy output, if 1950–60 trends continue, or the world reaches a level of consumption averaging a little above that of Western Europe in 1960.
3. Perhaps a five-fold increase in output of iron ore and ferroalloys, and somewhat less in copper, but a much larger increase in bauxite-aluminum.
4. A possible quadrupling of lumber output.

[1] A rough idea of how much more may be suggested by Figure 6 which indicates that approximately a 200 per cent increase in the value of the diet is needed to bring the hungry ⅔ of the world's people up to a Western Europe 1959–60 standard. This is equal to a 100 per cent increase for the world as a whole. A 100 per cent rise in food supplies for a population increased by 130 per cent would require an increase in food output of 360 per cent. These increases may be compared with the "target" of a 25 per cent per capita increase, considered by the FAO in its recent *Possibilities of Increasing World Food Production* (Rome, 1963). Using the U.N. "medium" population projection of 6,280 million for the year 2000, the FAO writer foresees the need for an increase in aggregate food output of 167 per cent (pp. 26–27); with the U.N. "high" projections used here, it would involve an increase of 188 per cent in aggregate output.

FOOD

The most important of these increases and the most difficult to meet is probably that in food output.

The chief hope of reaching the food "target"—unless important new technologies are developed, such as synthesizing foods from cellulose or petroleum, or getting acceptable food from algae—lies in increasing crop yields per acre. The first three columns of Table 14 show increases in yields for some of the principal crops as estimated by the FAO for the period of the 1950's. The average increase in yields on a world basis from these crops, chiefly grains, was something like 25 per cent for the decade. Thus, increases in yields per acre seem to account for most of the increase of 35 per cent in the total food output for this decade, as estimated by the FAO.[2] A 25 per cent per decade increase, if it were maintained for forty years, would raise the output of food and feed crops about 140 per cent—well over half the increase needed to triple output.

If, instead of extrapolating the world trends in increased yields for the 1950's, we consider what would be possible if the rate of progress in Europe and Northern America were extended worldwide and continued to the year 2000, we get much larger possibilities. Table 14 shows rates of increases in yields per acre running at 33 per cent and higher for the important grain crops in this area of the world. If such a rate of improvement were maintained by the entire world for four decades, the aggregate increase in crop output would be 210 per cent, which is more than the tripling sought to provide adequate calories.

[2] *State of Food and Agriculture 1962* (Rome: The Food and Agriculture Organization), p. 14. It should be noted that mainland China is included in the estimates of yields, while the estimates of total food output exclude China.

Reserves and Alternate Supply Possibilities

TABLE 14. Changes in Crop Yields per Acre, by Major Crops for Selected World Areas

	Percentage of increase in yields 1960–61 over 1948–49 to 1952–53			Yields in N. America and Europe ÷ Asia, Latin America, and Africa (1960)
	World	Europe	Northern America	
Wheat	22	25	42	1.99
Rye	29	20	53	1.95
Barley	31	45	11	2.28
Oats	19	21	23	1.93
Maize	29	80	37	2.83
Millet and sorghum	43	a	107	4.5
Rice	24	−4	52	2.3
Potatoes	5	13	29	1.8
Sweet potatoes and yams	−3	a	53	1.0
Cotton	33	a	56	2.3

a - very small quantities produced.
Source: FAO, Production Yearbook 1961, Tables 10A and 10B.

It might be possible that world agriculture could not only increase its yields at the same rate as Europe and Northern America, but that it might catch up with these advanced countries in yield per acre. The last column of Table 14 shows yields in the advanced countries at about double the levels in Asia, Africa, and Latin America, whose acreage is about 60 per cent of the total in the non-Communist world. If this 60 per cent doubled its yields, the output of the non-Communist world would increase 60 per cent; if the world also increased its yields each decade by 33 per cent of the European-American level, the total crop output in the year 2000 would be five times that in 1960. Such large increases in yields could not only provide the larger population with an adequate supply of calories, but offer a very large increase in the grain available for animal feed, as an aid in securing human diets with more proteins.

Crop production may be increased by increasing the acreage, as well as by increasing the yield per acre. The FAO *Production Yearbook* for 1961[3] reports about 350 million hectares (one hectare is equal to 2.2 acres) as "unused but potentially productive." This is about 25 per cent of the 1,409 million hectares listed as arable and under crops.[4] A 25 per cent increased area, yielding five times as much per acre (as supposed above), would yield a total increase in output of 525 per cent—over six times the 1960 total. To take another example, a 25 per cent increase in world acreage, yielding approximately as much as the European-American 1960 average on each acre, would give the world twice as much crop output as in 1960—a decrease in crop output per capita, in the light of the projected 130 per cent increase in world population between 1960 and 2000.

Although most experts believe that the greatest possibilities for solving the food problem lie in the direction of continuing increases in yields, there are large additional acreages which may be cultivated when sufficient need, ingenuity, or investment is brought to bear. The FAO tables list 4,000 million hectares as "forested"; 2,600 million hectares of "permanent meadows and pastures"; and over 5,000 million hectares of "built-on areas, wasteland, and other." Little more than 10 per cent of the world's land area is under crops. We may reasonably hope for substantial increases in the raising of crops on the more favorable parts of the remaining 90 per cent. Some of this may be at

---

[3] Table 1.

[4] Walter H. Pawley, in FAO's *Possibilities of Increasing World Food Production* (Rome, 1963), pp. 30–31, cites "reputable geographers" who have estimated the possibilities of increasing cultivated land as ranging from 35 per cent to 300 per cent.

the expense of pasture and timber land, thus diminishing the base for supplies of livestock products and lumber. But greater yields can also be obtained from the land which remains in pasture or timber, through the application of technology and investment.[5]

What is required to achieve the large increases in yields considered above? The matter is complex and includes some relatively unchangeable factors like climate and soil qualities; but large possibilities seem to center on the use of more adequate amounts of fertilizer, improved cultivation and harvesting practices, proper use of irrigation water, better drainage and soil demineralization, and use of better seeds and pesticides. More efficient tenure, credit, and marketing arrangements can also play an important part. Some of these factors, such as more fertilizer, require significant amounts of capital investment; others require institutional changes that may be even more difficult to achieve. Better extension services and a willingness to change long established farming practices can also make significant contributions.[6]

---

[5] *Timber Resources for America's Future* (U.S. Forest Service, 1958), pp. 476ff., indicated that nearly a four-fold increase in output was possible in the United States through better management alone. R. O. Whyte, T. R. G. Moir, and J. P. Cooper, in *Grasses in Agriculture* (FAO, Rome, 1959), state on page 4: "The great future development of grassland agronomy as such is likely to take place in the tropical and subtropical regions where the potentials are considered to be enormous and increases in yield of the order of 100, 200, or 300 percent may be obtained by simple adjustments in management or the application of fertilizer." The experts of the U.S. Department of Agriculture in 1960 foresaw a larger percentage yield increase for pasturage between 1958 and 1975 than for any of the major crops (*Our Farm Production Potential, 1975*, Agriculture Information Bulletin No. 233, Table 1). See also A. T. Semple, *Improving the World's Grasslands*, an FAO Study (London: Leonard Hill Ltd., 1952), p. 2, and *passim;* and *Latin American Timber Trends and Prospects* (FAO, 1963), pp. 82–86.

[6] See, for extensive discussion of techniques and possibilities in this field, *Possibilities of Increasing World Food Production*, FAO Freedom from Hunger Campaign basic study No. 10 (Rome, 1963).

Of these several factors, only water and fertilizer seem to present questions of the availability of resources. Water will probably continue to be a limiting factor in arid areas. Data are very limited, but a few generalizations are attempted later on in this chapter. With fertilizer, however, there seems to be no problem of availability, though the investments required for manufacture will be large. Reserves of presently usable phosphates and potash salts already known amount to about 50 billion tons each,[7] and the chief source of nitrogen is the practically infinite supply in the atmosphere. Against these supplies we may place estimates of 150–200 million tons[8] aggregate annual requirements for the food outputs projected above. This gives an estimate of 700 to 1,000 years' supply of phosphate and potash fertilizer at the year 2000 rate of use.

These calculations do not take into account another source of increase in the food supply, namely animal products. Increases in yields of output per animal would be in *addition* to those given here for crops, since our discussion has implicitly assumed that no gains are made in the effi-

---

[7] U.S. Bureau of Mines, *Mineral Facts and Problems,* 1960 edition, pp. 636, 655.

[8] This range is a crude approximation based on: (1) A FAO estimate of 70 million tons required to increase food output to an index of 175 (1960 = 100) by 1980 without increasing acres under cultivation. If output is to be increased to an index of 300, fertilizer requirements would probably increase more than in proportion, or to over 150 million tons, as compared to 1959–60 consumption of 27 million tons. (2) The high estimate, 200 million tons, is based on giving all countries a per capita fertilizer supply larger than the 1959/60 use in the developed countries (55 pounds).

Precise estimates would require an enormous amount of information to evaluate regional soil deficiencies, the gains in output to be expected from improved seeds, increased areas under cultivation, more irrigation and drainage, better harvesting methods, insecticides, etc. We shall be content here with very rough estimates.

See FAO, *Fertilizers and Economic Development,* by F. W. Parker, especially pp. 16–24.

ciency of conversion of grains and forage into animal products. The large gains which have already occurred in the advanced countries indicate that outputs per unit of feed can be greatly increased; and the large differences between the yields in the underdeveloped countries and those in the developed areas point to an additional source of large contributions to the world's food supplies.

The contribution which the world's fisheries can make to better diets has never been adequately explored, but it is undoubtedly also large. In 1961, about 23 per cent of the world's catch went into fertilizer and feed,[9] while many edible species went uncaught because they were not regarded as fit to eat. Some potentially rich fishing grounds in the Indian Ocean and off the west coast of Africa are hardly exploited at all, while others are probably fished far below their sustainable yields. Finally, much might be gained by breeding and caring for fish, for most species are still part of the primitive economy of free, competitive hunting.

Our projections implicitly assume that fish foods will increase in proportion to other foods, or that other foods will increase sufficiently to replace them. Since fish at present supply only about 10 per cent[10] of the world's animal protein, and 1 per cent of total foods, their replacement by animal products should not be too difficult, if it should prove necessary or desirable. It is possible, however, that output and consumption of fish will increase more than proportionately to other foods and make an important contribution to food supplies in the year 2000, above and beyond that assumed by our implicit projection.

[9] FAO, *Yearbook of Fishery Statistics 1961*, p. e–3.
[10] FAO, *Possibilities of Increasing World Food Production*, p. 190.

ENERGY

The problem of increasing energy output is complicated by the fact that mineral fuels are wasting assets; that is, there are fixed quantities in existence and replenishment is at a geological pace, infinitesimally slow relative to the rate of use. Knowledge of reserves is quite scanty, chiefly because there is insufficient incentive to do expensive exploration work until there is prospective use or market within the next one to three decades. All future values in the market place are subject to discount at the going rate of interest; a 5 per cent rate of discount makes a dollar fifty years hence worth only 9 cents today.

Speculative estimates, based on general knowledge of geological formations around the world, and on rates of occurrence of coal seams, oil and gas fields, and oil shale, indicate conventional energy resources equal to about 900 years of use at the 1960 rate of consumption, or 150–200 years of consumption at the rate we have projected for the year 2000.[11] Some investigators note that this does not include all discoveries which may be expected; if these are included total energy reserves might be four or five times as great.[12] Others regard such a 200-year forecast as optimistic, or at least they anticipate that many areas of the world will have to rely mainly on nuclear energy in less than a century if steeply increased costs and reductions in consumption are to be avoided.[13] In either case, the problem of

---

[11] *Fossil Fuels in the Future*, by Milton F. Searl (U.S. Atomic Energy Commission, October 1960), pp. 1–9; Sam H. Schurr, "Energy" in *Scientific American*, September 1963, p. 114.

[12] Cf. Schurr, *ibid.*, p. 116.

[13] H. J. Bhabha, Chairman, Indian Atomic Energy Commission, address at the U.N. Conference on Applications of Science and Technology for the Benefit of Less Developed Countries, Geneva, 1963.

Reserves and Alternate Supply Possibilities 59

any absolute world energy shortage is not foreseen until long after the year 2000.

Long before world shortages arise in fossil fuels, of course, atomic plants will be used for substantial amounts of energy. By the year 2000, 10 to 20 per cent of the world's energy consumption may come from atomic sources, principally as heating elements for the generation of electricity.[14] How adequate are the reserves of atomic fuels?

The U.S. Geological Survey is reported to have estimated potential uranium resources in this country, comparable in quality to ore now being mined, as representing more than twice the energy equivalent of all coal, oil, and gas resources now believed to exist in the country; by geological inference, the total energy content of world resources of currently minable uranium should also be larger than that of the fossil fuels.[15] This favorable view depends on the assumption that through "breeder" reactors it will be possible to convert the relatively abundant uranium 238 into fissionable plutonium. Further possibilities of abundant energy lie in the conversion of thorium into a fissionable material, and in the development of processes for exploiting lower grade ores. If an atomic fusion process is developed to a practical stage, much greater abundance will be available.

Between now and 2000, therefore, more than sufficient high-grade uranium and thorium ore would appear to be available to meet projected demands of the order of 10 to 20

---

[14] Projections made recently for the United States show that by 2000 about 15 per cent of total energy may come from nuclear sources, and about half of all electricity generation. From then on nuclear energy is expected to furnish increasing proportions of both. See Hans H. Landsberg, Leonard L. Fischman, Joseph L. Fisher, *Resources in America's Future* (Baltimore: The Johns Hopkins Press for Resources for the Future, 1963), pp. 282–92, 855, 858.

[15] Sam H. Schurr, "Energy," *op. cit.*, pp. 120–24.

per cent of total energy. The principal difficulties concern reactor technology and economies, safety, and, for less developed countries, capital requirements.

METALLIC MINERALS[16]

As we have observed previously, discovery and "proving up" of reserves of minerals is rarely done for more than will be required within two or three decades. However, enough is known in a rough sort of way to provide fair degrees of assurance for supplies at least as far as the year 2000.

A recent study indicates that for iron, aluminum, and manganese the known and inferred reserves are large enough, worldwide, to supply projected demands for at least the next forty years without significant increase in costs.[17] Doubts about the existence of unknown or inferred reserves may be moderated by noting that in recent years major new sources of iron ore, for example, have been discovered in Venezuela, Canada, Liberia, Brazil, and Australia, as well as other places. Techniques for beneficiating lower grade ores have also been improved. For copper, lead, and zinc, however, the demands which we have projected are expected to exhaust presently known and inferred reserves by the year 2000. Either large new discoveries of ore bodies or considerable advances in technology will be necessary to take care of the increased demands which will be experienced if anything like the 1950–60 rate of growth continues. It should be kept in mind, however, that there are satisfactory substitutes for these metals in most uses, and

[16] Fertilizer materials are discussed in connection with the preceding review of food potentials (p. 56).
[17] Bruce C. Netschert and Hans H. Landsberg, *The Future Supply of the Major Metals: A Reconnaissance Survey* (Resources for the Future, 1961).

that substitution, technology, and probably discovery will proceed at an accelerated pace if costs and prices rise.

FOREST PRODUCTS

Whether the world's forests will be able to stand the drains projected in Chapter 4 seems dubious, though much more information is required to make a conclusive judgment. We do know, however, that in the United States the relative price of lumber has risen by 300 per cent since 1870; and the U.S. Forest Service has warned that the projected rate of cutting trees of sawtimber grade over the next forty years considerably exceeds anticipated growth.[18]

International trade in lumber, pulp, and paper has been extensive and can be expected to continue so; consequently the world outlook is important for most countries, except for those with poor indigenous forests and little capacity to import forest products.

On the world scene, there is an encouraging sign. Data on land use indicate that half the world's output of sawlogs and 40 per cent of its total wood came from Northern America and Western Europe in 1960; yet the forested acreage in these two areas is only a little over 20 per cent of the world's total.[19] Thus, if sustained output in the rest of the world could be brought to a European-American level, output could be doubled. Such an increase, even so, would be substantially less than the tripling or quadrupling which a continuation of the postwar consumption trend would require. However, substitute materials are available; for example, steel, aluminum, fiberboard, and building blocks.

[18] *Timber in America's Future* (U.S. Government Printing Office, 1958), especially pp. 96ff.
[19] FAO, *Production Yearbook 1961*, Table 1.

The physical potentials for hardwoods in tropical areas are known to be great, but the problems of economic exploitation are most difficult.

Changes in management practices that would entail only moderate costs could yield a large increase even in United States output, especially in small private holdings.[20] In less developed areas, where cutting practices are poorer than in this country, the gains from this source could be much greater.

WATER

Thus far in this study we have not gone into the outlook for water demand and supply for either the United States or the whole world. This is only because comprehensive historical data for the United States are limited; and for many parts of the world virtually nonexistent. Lack of data is among the most pressing problems in the water resource field. The high cost of supplying fresh water severely limits economic development in many arid and semiarid areas. Precipitation is irregular in most countries, both regionally and seasonally, and water is costly to transport, prohibitively so for long distances.

Estimates of water demand and supply by continents, or even by countries except for the very smallest, make little sense; the job has to be done by river basins and frequently by portions of basins. However, some rough estimates made recently for the United States indicate that withdrawal uses —by cities, industries, and irrigation farmers—have been rising fairly rapidly and will continue to do so in the future.

---

[20] See Charles H. Stoddard, *The Small Private Forest in the United States* (Resources for the Future, 1961).

In the East withdrawal depletions (the fresh water taken from streams and lakes and not returned) are projected to increase from 14 billion gallons per day in 1960 to 37 billion in 2000; in the more arid West from 60 to 92 billion gallons per day, and in the Pacific Northwest from 11 to 20 billion gallons per day.[21] Large additional amounts of water, not actually depleted but frequently rendered unavailable for other uses, will be required to dilute pollutants and carry them downstream. In the arid West, lack of enough water could limit further expansion in agriculture; industrial growth in some areas might be blocked unless a larger share of the water supply is allocated to this use. In the East and in metropolitan and industrial regions, generally the chief problems are those of water quality.

A number of possibilities exist for augmenting supplies. Additional storage reservoirs can be constructed; evaporation and irrigation canal losses can be checked; water-consuming trees and plants can be reduced; water can be recycled in industry; salt or brackish water can be substituted for fresh water in cooling and some other uses; water prices can be raised to check increases in consumption; surface and groundwater sources can be integrated for more economic use; whole river systems can be interconnected. Brackish and even ocean water can be demineralized by several different methods at costs which in a few remote places are already competitive with those for fresh water from other sources. Pollution abatement on many streams would yield large amounts of higher quality and, therefore, more usable water than is now available. Large gains could be made by legal and institutional changes which would result in some reallocation of water use away from irrigation, toward in-

---

[21] Landsberg, Fischman, Fisher, *op. cit.*, p. 28.

dustrial and other much higher value uses. For the United States, speaking generally, water requirements for the next four decades can probably be met, save for a few places, if a number of these supply-increasing and loss-reducing efforts are applied with reasonable success.

Western Europe, also a highly developed area, for the most part has ample rainfall so that with additional investment and careful management future needs of a relatively slow-growing population should be met. The same appears to be true for Japan, although in both these areas development will have to be intensive and management more careful. More effective institutional arrangements than in the United States have made possible heavy concentrations of population and water-using industries in the Ruhr valley of West Germany, despite limited amounts of fresh water.[22]

For the less developed areas information is still more scanty.[23] Obviously water is short in some places and at some periods of the year, while it is too plentiful in other places and times. In many of the more arid areas, such as West Pakistan, North Africa, and Northeast Brazil, agricultural improvement will depend heavily on water developments of various kinds. Cheap demineralization obviously would be a boon in such places as these; to date costs by various feasible methods are still much too high to permit large-scale application. However, for human consumption in a few high-cost places demineralized water is already being produced. Some fifty water-short areas in various parts of

---

[22] Allen V. Kneese, "Water Quality Management by Regional Authorities in the Ruhr Area," *Proceedings of the Regional Science Association*, December 1962.

[23] Irving K. Fox, "Water Resources of the World," *Federation Proceedings,* Fifth International Congress on Nutrition (Baltimore: Federation of American Societies for Experimental Biology, Vol. 20, No. 1, March 1961), pp. 378–80.

Reserves and Alternate Supply Possibilities 65

the world have been identified recently in which technical and economic studies appear warranted to determine the possibilities for utilization of desalinated water.[24]

By and large, requirements for the next few decades at least can probably be met in most areas of the world provided necessary investments are made and water is used with increasing efficiency; in certain arid or water-deficient areas economic development undoubtedly will be hampered, perhaps checked entirely, by lack of usable water.

[24] See *Water Desalinization in Developing Countries* (New York: United Nations, 1964).

CHAPTER 6

Some Concluding Observations

In this study we have tried to marshal what statistical evidence we could readily find to shed light on the important question: Are resources becoming scarcer in the United States and the world? The picture that emerges is not simple and clear-cut. Limiting our forward look to the year 2000, we find no general increase in scarcity in the more developed areas; the opposite trend is likely to continue. In the less developed areas severe problems will be encountered, but the situation is not hopeless. Much will depend on policies both in the aid-receiving and the aid-giving countries, and on the international economic and political climate generally. Most important will be the effort put forth and the competence of people in the less developed countries in dealing with their resource problems and potentials.

For the United States, historical data have been assembled and systematic projections made to the year 2000. The U.S. historical data do not point to increasing scarcity in any general sense. Indications as to future technology and supply possibilities, when matched against projected demands for the next four decades, likewise do not indicate a general tendency toward increase in scarcity. A continued rise in the material level of living seems assured. This does not mean there will not be supply problems for particular re-

Some Concluding Observations

sources at particular times and places; rather it means that in this country technological and economic progress, building upon an ample and diversified resource and industrial base, gives assurance that supply problems can be met. If this rather favorable prognosis is to be guaranteed in fact, scientific and technological advance will have to continue unabated and the results will have to be translated into economic reality. In addition, it will be essential to extend, or at least maintain to the present degree, a world trading and investing system in which raw material deficits can be met through imports from other countries with a surplus of these materials. Any devastating war would, of course, throw off all of the projections undertaken here as well as conclusions drawn from them.

The historical data for most of the world, particularly the less developed areas, are not extensive or reliable enough to support more than highly tentative conclusions regarding long-range future adequacy of natural resources and raw materials. We have examined such evidence as we could readily find. For the more developed countries, particularly in Western Europe, where the data are reasonably good, the trend is not unlike that for the United States, according to the historical evidence and the projections we have made. The importance of a viable world trading system is, if anything, greater for most of the other more developed countries than for the United States since they tend to rely more heavily on raw material imports and upon exports of processed goods and services in exchange for them. The success of the European Common Market and the European Coal and Steel Community over recent years is an indication of the importance of widening the area of freer trade.

In the less developed areas of the world, the data are extremely thin; projections are hazardous. One simply does not know enough about historical trends to gauge the rapidity with which technical advances already made in the more developed countries will be applied widely in the less developed ones. Nor can population projections be relied upon as coming very close to what will actually happen.

Nevertheless, we have speculated on possibilities of future resource demand and supply in the less developed countries in the preceding two chapters of this inquiry. We are not persuaded that the next few decades will see any general or marked deterioration of living levels because of increasing scarcity of raw materials; on the other hand, prospective rates of population increase are high in many countries and do not afford much assurance that living levels can be increased very rapidly. We venture the view that living levels in most countries can increase over the coming years, with diets improving slowly and energy and mineral use more rapidly. The process depends heavily on education, motivation, favorable government policies, and social adaptations. We do not believe that shortages and inadequacies of natural resources and raw materials are likely to make modest improvements in levels of living impossible of achievement.

It is nevertheless likely that a slower rate of population increase, due to a decline in the birth rate, would be associated with a faster increase in per capita levels of living. In this event the population would contain a smaller percentage of children and a larger percentage of persons in the working ages; there would be fewer mouths to feed compared with hands to work; and it would be easier to increase the proportion of invested capital to labor.

We must reiterate here that we have examined the future only as far as the year 2000. Projecting population growth beyond that at, say, 2 per cent per year soon leads to very high figures—12 to 15 billion by 2040, 25 to 30 billion by

Some Concluding Observations

2080, and so on. That the resource base of the world could accommodate such growth for more than a century is open to serious question. Of course, technology would not stand still either, and one must not underestimate the capacity of individuals and social institutions to respond intelligently and constructively to emerging problems, even though one cannot see exactly when or how such adaptations will be made. Increasing knowledge of reproduction physiology, advances in birth control techniques, and changing attitudes toward family planning may combine to check present population growth rates long before there is "standing room only."

There are certain escape hatches from any tendency toward increasing scarcity, and it is important that these be kept open. In fact, the challenge of public policy and private management of resource enterprises is to keep them open, both in developed and less developed countries. Among the ways of staving off or mitigating resource scarcity are the following:

1. Possibilities for substitution of a more plentiful, convenient, and cheaper material for one that is becoming scarcer (that is, rising in cost and price) will usually exist. The more diversified a country's technology, industry, and labor force, the more readily substitutions can be made. For example, in the United States over the past forty years there have been massive substitutions within such categories as building materials, metal alloys, foods, and fuels. Sometimes the impulse toward substitution arises from raw material level, perhaps because of the discovery of a new source; sometimes it arises at the final consumer end, as when a family decides to switch from one finished item to another; and sometimes a change at an intermediate

level of processing triggers the substitution. In each case the implication for the resource materials may be considerable: some of the changes may be resource-saving and some resource-using, frequently saving for a scarcer resource and using for a more plentiful one.

2. An escape hatch of increasing importance in the resource field is the application of more than one use to a given basic resource such as land or water. The larger economies and benefits to be secured from the multiple-purpose development and use of a river system have long been well established, and now are being realized in development programs in many less developed countries. Use of water for irrigation, flood control, navigation, and hydroelectric power are now being combined with "new" purposes such as outdoor recreation, dilution of pollutants, and new industrial processes. Similarly, for land it will be increasingly desirable to develop and manage large tracts for multiple purposes of forest products production, animal grazing, agriculture, outdoor recreation, and to some extent for planned urban development.

3. Yet another escape hatch, at least when the matter is viewed from the point of view of a particular country, is the importing of needed or cheaper raw materials from elsewhere. The United States in about 1930 shifted from being a net exporter of resource materials to a position of net importer, where it has remained ever since. This country is still a large exporter of wheat, cotton, and certain other raw materials, principally agricultural, and a net importer of crude oil, iron ore, copper, lead, zinc, bauxite, and many other mineral raw materials. Many of the less developed countries depend heavily upon exports of mineral and

agricultural raw materials, and imports of yet other resource products. Increasingly, most countries of the world will find it advantageous to their own development if a viable world trading and investment system can be maintained so that high-cost programs of national sufficiency will not be necessary. The more effectively such a system operates, the more productive the whole world economy will become, and the more chance there will be that tendencies toward shortage in particular countries can be checked.

4. Programs of resource research, conservation, development, and better management can also contribute to the avoidance of incipient tendencies toward scarcity. Frequently these need to be planned and integrated for particular regions. For example, in West Pakistan, the better management of water used in agriculture could greatly increase yields and hence levels of food consumption. Such a program would involve agricultural land drainage and demineralization along with the application of more and better fertilizers, more efficient farm management, and many other changes.[1] In some instances public and private policies of conservation (by which is usually meant the shifting of the rate of use of a resource from the present toward the future) will be desirable as a part of national and regional development programs. For example, in selected instances the postponement of timber cutting or the catching of fish until the stock and growth rate are at more favorable levels will be helpful. Conservation, in

[1] Joseph L. Fisher and Roger Revelle, "Natural Resources Policies and Planning for Developing Countries,' in Vol. I, *Natural Resources: Energy, Water and River Basin Development*, U.S. papers prepared for the U.N. Conference on the Application of Science and Technology for the Benefit of the Less Developed Areas (Washington: U.S. Government Printing Office, 1963).

the sense of reduction of waste at various stages between initial development of the resource and final consumption of its products, frequently will prove to be economic and can make an important contribution to the avoidance of shortage. Resources research and development programs will have to be pursued vigorously if new sources of resource materials are to be found and cheaper substitutes are to be forthcoming. Without sufficient research and development any optimism about the future would quickly vanish; with effective research and development even stubborn problems can be made to yield.

It can be seen from these various observations regarding the central question of whether resources are becoming scarcer, that much of the answer will lie outside the resource industries and activities themselves. General programs of education and more specialized programs for training scientists, technical personnel, and managers will be important. The capacity of people in less developed countries to make use of technological improvements already successfully demonstrated in more developed areas will be of particular significance. Social organization and willingness to experiment with new policies frequently will determine whether or not a country will be successful in its development and use of natural resources. For example, land tenure arrangements, laws and customs regarding the ownership and use of water, and willingness to try out new agricultural and forest management techniques are of great significance. Institutions which make possible rapid transfer of knowledge and techniques from more to less developed areas should be given special attention. Extension service activities will be of critical importance.

Some Concluding Observations

It would appear desirable to initiate and maintain on a world scale a continuing estimate of growing demand for resources and raw materials, a continuing inventory of reserves and potential supplies at various levels of cost, and an indicated matching of demands and supplies as a result of various technological innovations, policies, and actions.[2]

A final observation: further investigation of past resource development and use trends will make it possible to project future situations more accurately. This study has attempted to bring together some of the more significant and readily available resource data as a basis for demand and supply projections for various major areas of the world. As more work is done along these lines, it should be possible to specify more clearly the emerging problems of scarcity so that farsighted corrective policies can be installed in advance of the onset of tight situations. As time goes on we should be able to answer with less and less indecision the central question as to whether resources are becoming scarcer over the world.

[2] Recent work of the U.N. Food and Agriculture Organization and the U.S. Department of Agriculture has gone far toward achieving this objective in the field of food, while the U.S. Geological Survey, the Bureau of Mines, and the Atomic Energy Commission have made excellent surveys of energy resources. In the field of energy, Resources for the Future has recently initiated a series of studies by which historical trends in the energy commodities will be examined on a world scale as a basis for making some projections of likely demand several decades into the future.

In this connection the establishment of a World Resource Development Institute has been proposed which, among other things, could sponsor comprehensive and systematic projections of resource demand and supply. See Fisher and Revelle, *ibid.*

DATE DUE

FEB 24 '72			
MAR 27 '72			
APR 24 '72			
MAR 22 '76			
APR 8 '76			
APR 15 '76			
APR 29 '76			
AP 12 '77			
DE 14 '79			
AP 21 '88			
GAYLORD			PRINTED IN U.S.A.